THE COMPLEAT
TAILDRAGGER PILOT

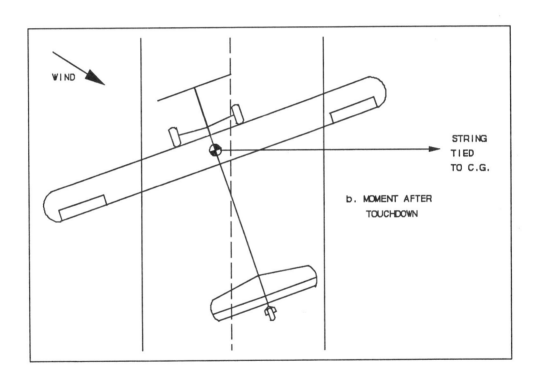

WIND

STRING
TIED
TO C.G.

b. MOMENT AFTER
TOUCHDOWN

by
HARVEY S. PLOURDE

NOTE OF CAUTION

The material in this book is based upon the author's personal experiences. The techniques described have been used successfully over an extensive period of time and in numerous airplane models by pilots willing to develop the necessary skills. Nevertheless, the book is not intended to replace instruction from and supervision by a qualified instructor. The author disclaims responsibility for any harm occuring to an individual who attempts to use any of the procedures described herein without first having acquired the requisite skills from a qualified and properly certificated flight instructor.

First printing November 1991
Second printing October 1992
Third printing May 1994
Fourth printing July 1996
Fifth printing June 1998
Sixth printing September 1998
Seventh printing April 2000
© Copyright by Harvey S. Plourde 1991

Published by and copies available from:

Muguette B. Plourde
5 Hermsdorf Ave.
Goffstown, NH 03045

Dedication

To my wife Muguette, who waited.

Table of Contents

THE COMPLEAT TAILDRAGGER PILOT

Table of Contents

THE COMPLEAT TAILDRAGGER PILOT

Table of Contents

Acknowledgements

This book began as a collection of notes used as handouts in the New Hampshire Wing of the Civil Air Patrol's numerous check-out programs, first in 1972 when the Cessna L-19 Birddog was introduced and later in 1975 when many of the pilots transitioned into the DeHavilland DHC-2 Beaver. The notes were amplified from the lively discussions which grew out of the many ground schools we held.

As the book grew, it became clear that many of the Civil Air Patrol pilots who had endured all those saturdays of "circuits and bumps" with me had contributed significantly if unwittingly. I thank all of them for the experience and camaraderie which they provided. In particular, I must thank LTC. Paul Teague, CAP, whom I have always been so proud to have shared the sky with. Also, I thank LTC. Calvin Stiles who, as Director of Operations for N.H. Wing, was always very supportive of my efforts.

Additionally, Mr. Donald Mathieson, CFI and experienced taildragger pilot took on the burden of reviewing the manuscript in its entirety. He provided many useful comments which resulted in definite improvements in the text. Likewise, Mr. Normand Bisson rendered valuable assistance with Appendix B in particular, and always made his encyclopedic knowledge of general aviation airplanes available to me. Finally, I also thank William K. Kershner and Tony Bingelis for the encouragement which they provided when I needed it most.

For many years, Mr. Demi Copadis was the Accident Prevention Specialist of the FAA's GADO 15 in Portland, Maine. Demi contributed to this book in many ways. His availability, knowledge, and professional bearing were always a credit to the Administration. But most importantly, Demi always understood the General Aviation pilot.

Lastly, I must thank all of the flight instructors whose patience I tested over the years. There were many. The overwhelming majority were outstanding. Still, I even managed to learn something from the the few who were not. So, from the familiar refrain,

"Bless 'em all,

The tall, the short, and the bald,

Bless all those instructors

Who taught me to fly............"

On many occasions when I needed a good textbook containing material on the subject of Taildraggers, I found that the existing texts were wanting. Older texts tend to contain a minimum of detail, and even some of that detail is indeed incorrect. Other books which are considered excellent for contemporary training, treat the taildragger very quickly and with a broad brush. Here again, there is insufficient detail. Other pilots in similar circumstances have found the same void, and have been frustrated by this lack of material. To be sure, we have articles purporting to be complete tutorials on taildragger flying published in the popular flying magazines on an annual basis. Unfortunately, the subject is too complex to adequately cover in the three or four pages allowed by the typical magazine editor, and these articles, as good as some are, merely scratch the surface. Hence the need for a comprehensive taildragger book existed.

The creation of this book began with notes written for various "Taildragger Conversion Ground Schools" which I was called on to teach over the past thirty years or so. Some of these were for the Civil Air Patrol, and others were for private individuals or groups. As each course was prepared, my notes tended to grow in order to allow me to address ("squeeze in" might be more appropriate wording) more detail. My own curiosity and engineering background led me to seek answers in areas which I could not find documented elsewhere. Hence, the curves on "torque", the analysis of P-Factor, and the chapter on Cross Wind Landing Gear came about. All of the techniques discussed were proven in the numerous hours of transition training and have withstood the test of time.

Finally, serious work on converting my notes into this book began in 1976, with progress being made sporadically in between numerous lengthy periods of inactivity.

If this book prevents a single taildragger accident or personal injury, my efforts will have borne fruit.

Harvey S. Plourde
Goffstown, New Hampshire
June, 1991

1

INTRODUCTION

It is a truism that taildraggers are getting scarcer all the time, especially since there are so few being manufactured today. At this writing, the combined production of the Christen Husky, the Piper Super-Cub, and the Maule series probably barely equals the number of taildraggers disposed of each year due to accidents, corrosion, etc..

Of equal concern is the shortage of proficient taildragger pilots, and the rapidly diminishing number of competent taildragger instructors.

The primary objective of this book is to assist in the preservation of those few taildraggers left as well as their pilots. There are two ways to prolong the longevity of the taildraggers, namely to fly them well, and to maintain them equally well. With the exception of a few comments in chapter 11, this book is not about maintenance.

This material is intended for the person wishing to learn more about taildragger flying than he or she already knows. That person does not have to be a pilot to read the book, however a background of aviation knowledge will help in the understanding of this material. The person most likely to make good use of this book is the pilot planning on a transition from tricycle geared airplanes to taildraggers regardless of pilot experience level. The beginning taildragger student will find a gold mine of information which will help reduce the number of hours necessary to learn a given maneuver. The experienced taildragger pilot, on the other hand, may still pick up some tidbits which will make him a safer pilot, or may gain an explanation of some procedure which he has been using for some time but which he never fully understood.

In view of the advanced average age of most of today's taildragger Flight Instructors and the need to continue producing instructors to replace them, a section of this book is devoted to the subject of planning and conducting a successful transition program from tricycle geared airplane to taildragger.

Finally, it will be interesting to any pilot whose curiosity has led him to wonder about the difference between conventional geared and tricycle geared airplanes and their attendant care and feeding. It is this curiosity which serves as a driving force for many of us and which sets the stage for most learning by the human animal.

The material in this book is presented in a manner which will not require continuous reading from start to finish. The reader interested in a given topic may go directly to the pertinent pages and concentrate attention there. Nevertheless, the reader desiring to learn the maximum will be well served by making a first pass through the book's entirety and then studying in greater detail the material in which in-depth-knowledge is desired. He can then use the book as a vehicle for discussions with his instructor over the topics which he wants to learn but doesn't readily understand.

Some of the material in the book may appear intimidating to the reader. Other portions of the material may take on the appearance of "scare" items. Neither of the above was intended, and the reader should take comfort in the fact that not all of the material needs to be understood by the pilot in order to successfully fly taildraggers. The evidence of that is in the thousands of pilots who originally learned to fly in taildraggers, many without an hour's ground school, and for whom a subject such as "torque" was nothing more than a vague force which could be corrected for by a quick right foot without the need for an engineering degree. Many of these pilots went on to fly some heavy hardware through both of our World Wars, and did it well.

One of the goals of the author in writing this book was to package as much taildragger information as reasonably possible within one set of covers. Hence, some of the material has appeared elsewhere or is general knowledge and is repeated here for reference. Added to that is material developed by the author and introduced in print for the first time. Still, in order to keep the book's length within reasonable bounds, we have not included material which is not specific to taildraggers. Thus, you will not find discussions of traffic patterns, cruise flight, X-C navigation etc. All of these can be found in readily available texts.

While it is understood that one cannot learn taildragger flying from a book any more than one can any other type of flying, the material in this text should allow the reader to make the transition much more safely and painlessly.

1   THE COMPLEAT TAILDRAGGER PILOT

All of the anecdotes mentioned herein are authentic and happened to the author or his students, and are included for purposes of illustration as well as to encourage the reader to learn from the mistakes of others.

When all is said and done, the pilot transitioning successfully to taildraggers will be amazed at the ease with which the airplane can be flown, and will do so with a great sense of pride.

May the book contribute to the preservation of the few taildraggers which we have left.

2

WARM UP

The person desiring to learn to fly taildraggers may wish to do so for a variety of different reasons. To some, the element of machismo which tends to surround the taildragger types at the local airport is enough to set them off in quest of lessons. Others may have more practical reasons covering the gamut from "my father owns a taildragger" to "I need the checkout to get the job I want towing banners". If we list as many of these reasons as come to mind, the list could look like the following:

1. Father (or relative or friend) owns a taildragger which the pilot wants to fly.

2. Local flying club which our pilot wants to join has only a taildragger.

3. Pilot has developed an interest in antique or warbird aircraft, and he has learned that the majority are taildraggers.

4. Pilot wants to take aerobatic lessons, and the only aerobatic airplane available to him is a taildragger.

5. Pilot needs the taildragger experience for a job field which he wants to enter. This could be Agricultural flying, banner towing, glider towing, or bush flying. The majority of these jobs are done in taildraggers.

6. Pilot may be shopping for a Homebuilt and plans to buy one of the taildragging variety. Or, our pilot has built a taildragger and is tired of watching his partner fly it.

7. Pilot has heard of the taildragger "challenge", and wants the feeling of accomplishment which accompanies good taildragger skills.

Perhaps the most likely reason to come along is the recent discovery that used taildragger prices are not escalating as high as the prices for comparable tricycle geared airplanes. Whatever the reason for this trend, it means that the capable pilot may save himself a significant portion of the purchase price by buying a taildragger.

Until recently, there was no FAA regulation requiring that a pilot's taildragger checkout be administered by a Certificated Flight Instructor. Indeed, the only place in the FAR's where taildraggers were specifically mentioned insofar as pilot requirements are concerned was in Paragraph 61.57 which states that the three takeoffs and landings required in the past 90 days must be in a tail wheel airplane and to a full stop if the recency of experience is to apply to tail wheel airplanes [1] . Hence, while a self checkout might

---

[1] See Appendix A for the full FAR Paragraph 61.57 (c)

not be a smart thing to do, it was nevertheless quite legal. Likewise, a checkout from a non-instructor pilot was also legal. This state of affairs was undoubtedly a holdover from the days when all pilots were taildragger pilots because taildraggers were the only airplanes available for instruction. Correspondingly, so were the instructors. This policy was fine for those days, but the advent of tricycle gear which became almost universally used in trainers resulted in the creation of many pilots and flight instructors without taildragger knowledge.

The accidents arising from this lack of proper regulation are not easily quantified, but apparently were sufficient to encourage a regulatory change. To be sure, many of the insurance companies had, for several years, required a CFI endorsement, but that only proves that it is the insurance companies who really control this country and not the government bureaucracy.

By the spring of 1991, the inertia had finally been overcome, and FAR 61.31 was modified to require a logbook endorsement from a CFI in order to legally fly the taildragger [2]. The only exception allowed is the usual grandfather clause for pilots with Pilot-in-command time in taildraggers prior to April 15, 1991. Perhaps the greatest benefit of the new regulation will be that the pilot transitioning to taildraggers will now be required to demonstrate competence in wheel landings. This will no doubt make the transition program

---

[2] As of this writing, FAR Part 61 has been revised to require taildragger pilots to have a check ride from a CFI, and a logbook endorsement attesting to the fact. See Appendix A for Par. 61.31 (g).

a bit longer, but will have the advantage of increasing the skill level of the pilots concerned. This will preclude the common practice of transitioning pilots who are having difficulties with the wheel landing. They tend to cut the transition short by informing the CFI that "I'll call you in a couple of weeks for some wheel landing practice", and the instructor never hears from them again. He now knows that another half-trained taildragger pilot is loose.

The presence of the new regulation now sends you in search of the instructor who will conduct and bless your transition. Here is how you should go about that search.

SELECTING AN INSTRUCTOR

The selection of a taildragger instructor should be weighed in favor of one with significant flight and teaching experience specifically in taildraggers. It is easy to fall into the trap of going to an instructor who has high time in tricycle geared airplanes and minimal time in taildraggers. He may try to convince you that "it doesn't make any difference, because airplanes are all the same". But history shows that this statement just isn't true. The instructor with 2000 hours who got a 2-hour checkout in a Citabria last month is not likely to be qualified to teach in taildraggers.

What should the minimum be? If a member of my family were the customer, I would insist that the instructor have a minimum of 100 hours P.I.C. plus an additional 100 hours of instruction given, all in taildraggers, and that at least 5 hours have been within the last 90 days. It would also be beneficial if his record included at least 20 hours in the specific model which you want your instruction in. Remember that the instructor has two primary functions. First, he is there to teach; secondly he must prevent any accident while you learn, and he can hardly accomplish this with only 10 or 15 hours of taildragger time. To be sure, time flown is not the only criterion for choosing an instructor, and you can certainly think of others. However, the minimums mentioned above are a good starting point.

PLANNING YOUR PROGRAM

Now that you've found an instructor whom you believe equal to the task ahead, a good skull session with your selection is advisable. An early question to ask is to have your instructor describe the flight as well as the ground portion of the program to you. The ground school is very important, especially if you believe one of flight instruction's oldest axioms, namely that "the airplane is the world's worst classroom; it is noisy, hot (or cold), expensive, and lacks a black-board". An adequate taildragger conversion ground school should span a minimum of 2 to 4 hours. (The lower figure for persons who have studied this text, and the greater number for those who haven't). And experience shows that each hour of class time will probably replace 1.5 hours of flight time which makes it a very good trade. If your instructor doesn't believe in ground school for this endeavor, you should perhaps keep on looking because you haven't found the right person yet.

The amount of flight time required for a taildragger transition will depend on a number of factors and is therefore more difficult to guesstimate. For example, it depends on the specific model to be used, wind conditions in your local area, your own reflexes, and most importantly, the number of tricycle gear bad habits which you will have to "unlearn" before you can expect to make progress. You can be sure of one thing, however, and that is that your indoctrination is likely to require more than just a couple of hours, with 10 hours being a reasonable minimum. The fallacious notion that the pilot transitioning to taildraggers only needs a couple of hours of takeoffs and landings and then can be turned loose to learn the rest on his own still persists in many quarters. When this is attempted, the result quickly arrived at is that the new pilot is quite comfortable in the airplane as long as the winds remain below 5 or 6 knots and within 20 degrees of the runway center line. Beyond that, the pilot quickly learns—to his chagrin—that he is in over his head and the flight ends with the sounds of crunching metal. The problem here is that in order for the pilot to survive severe crosswinds, some of his training must take place in those conditions. Any less is seriously short changing the student. This "just a couple hours" advice often comes from the local "airport bum", a taildragger pilot himself with sadistic tendencies, who will quietly observe from behind the farthest corner of the hangar while laughing at the wild results. His kind of advice is to be avoided like the plague.

If you have a choice, stack the deck in your favor by your selection of airplane and the type of runway surface to use for the instruction. In the former case, you may wish to fly your recently purchased classic Cessna 195, but will find the learning process infinitely shorter and more comfortable if you start in a Piper J-3 Cub. There are many types suitable for a taildragger introduction among which any of the following have a history of good service. These are the aforementioned Cub and the various Super Cub variations, Taylorcraft, Aeronca Champ or Chief, Citabria, Luscombe, Cessna 120 and 140 series, Porterfield, and Interstate. Any of these will teach you the taildragger principles which you can then carry on to the larger airplanes. The main advantage of proceeding in this way is that these airplanes were originally designed and built for the training role, and consequently are much more forgiving of poor handling.

In the second case, make grass your choice of runway surface if it is available (even if you have to drive or fly a greater distance for your lessons). The forgiveness inherent in a grass surface especially if the grass is wet has to be experienced in order to be believed. The wet grass will often allow a light airplane landing with a slight drift to escape with nothing more than a shrug, whereas the same error indulged in on a hard surface would most likely result in a ground-loop with attendant damage of the airplane.

Continuing this line of thinking soon convinces us that the best of both worlds, from a training viewpoint, would be a field with a grass strip alongside the paved runway. The training could then start on grass, move to the hard surface when the winds are benign, return to the grass for crosswind training, then finish the lessons with crosswinds on the asphalt. This would provide the optimum learning with the maximum insurance against damage. Alas, such airports are scarce.

LIMITATIONS—YOURS AND THE AIRPLANE'S

There is a popular notion in taildragger flying circles which has contributed to the destruction of many taildraggers. This is the belief that "a good taildragger pilot can operate in any wind in which a tricycle geared airplane can be flown". While it is a fact that a good pilot can handle a lot of wind in a taildragger, the same pilot, because of his taildragger honed skills, can handle much stronger wind situations in tricycle gear. The fundamental reason why a taildragger cannot be flown in winds as strong as the tricycle gear can be is the huge angle of attack which the airplane has while sitting on the ground in a three point attitude. If we compare similar airplanes such as the Cessna 170 and its tricycle geared counterpart, the 172 as flown by equally proficient pilots, we would probably find that the 170 pilot has to give up in the presence of crosswinds gusting to 18-23 knots, while his friend may be able to handle 28 knots of the same. (This is not meant as a recommendation, but as an example).

If you doubt the above, speak with an old FBO, by that we mean one who's living depended on renting out taildraggers in the days when there was no other type in use. Listen to him tell you how they had to shut the rental business down at 2:00 o'clock on so many windy afternoons. The advent of the tricycle gear was to the FBO that which the jet was to the airlines. It made the difference, and put their businesses into the black for the first time.

Now that you understand the airplane's limitation, give some thought to your own limitations such as they will be for some time in the future. Bear in mind that, even though your flying time may add up to several thousand hours, you are still a rookie as far as the taildragger is concerned. Hence, your gaze at the wind sock should be through the eyes of a student. While the hours behind you may help you to learn more quickly, this learning process must still be experienced.

At this point it would be well for you to review your proposed training program with your instructor and obtain his confirmation that you will obtain windy day experience (when you are ready for it), and that wheel landings will be part of the curriculum. If he asks you why you think you will need training in making wheel landings, you should continue pursuing your request with your intention being to get his feeling on the subject.

Some pilots converted to taildraggers are convinced that they don't need to learn or practice wheel landings because three-point landings are "just as good". The pilot who believes this is seriously short changing himself, and won't realize his error until he finds himself attempting a landing in 15 - 18 knot gusting crosswinds. The reason that wheel landing training is mandatory is that it allows the pilot to place the landing gear on the ground with a lower angle of attack and higher speed, hence with a greater degree of control. It is of course natural for a beginning taildragger pilot to not understand this need. However, if your instructor shares this line of thinking, consider yourself lucky to have made the discovery, and keep on looking. Until the taildragger pilot can perform acceptable wheel landings, he should consider himself at the student level (regardless of how many hours grace his logbook), and stay close to his instructor where his solo flying can be supervised.

2 THE COMPLEAT TAILDRAGGER PILOT

MISCONCEPTIONS

Finally, before we leave this section, let's look at a couple of extreme yet very common opinions and see if we can separate the wheat from the chaff.

The first is that "taildragger pilots are not necessarily better pilots". This statement appears in print in many of the popular aviation magazines with amazing regularity. It may sell magazines, but it can easily lead to accidents by implying that the tricycle gear pilot could perform a self taught transition to taildraggers. To state the requirement accurately, let's simply say that the taildragger is more difficult to fly than a tricycle geared airplane due to the fact that the pilot must cancel all sideways motion with respect to the ground at the moment of touchdown. The difficulty in the procedure of canceling sideways drift depends of course on the crosswind velocity and its variability as manifested by gusts. The taildragger pilot must, if he is going to remain accident-free, develop the ability to read the wind constantly to the point where it becomes subconscious. He must also cultivate manipulative skills with the controls which the tri-gear pilot will never use. Each time the taildragger pilot takes off and lands in a strong crosswind he's betting his career and his airplane that he is a better pilot.

The average tricycle gear pilot believes that he also is doing this at every landing, but a few hours watching the takeoffs and landings at your local airport will prove to you the fallacy of that belief. The difference is that the tricycle geared airplane is so forgiving that it can survive a fair amount of drift at touchdown.

As in other areas of life, excessive forgiveness leads to a great deal of sin. And the typical tricycle gear pilot finds himself spending less and less effort trying to cancel all drift in his landings. The result is the development of a bad habit which could be disastrous in taildraggers. Such is the stuff from which accidents are made. In short, for reasons which we will see in the next section, the taildragger is much more sensitive to pilot error than the nosedragger. The proof of this is the large number of tricycle geared airplanes built since the early 1950's. Even though they are more expensive to build than taildraggers and provide slightly degraded performance, they have been built because they increase the hours of operation of the FBO, and that makes the difference between economic survival and bankruptcy.

The flip side of this coin is the fallacy perpetuated by taildragger pilots that only a rare form of superman can survive in the devious machine. This is an exaggeration on a grand scale. What the pilot needs is good training and enough supervised practice to hone his newly acquired skills in a variety of wind conditions. This last, the "variety of wind conditions" is the element too often missing in the training of pilots. In the days when the only airplanes around were taildraggers, we still had numerous ham-handed pilots who survived. They were not Supermen. Likewise, I have also known several top notch lady taildragger drivers so that (except for a few cases which we will discuss on an individual basis later) there is no reason why the Ms. or Mrs. pilots cannot do their share of taildragger flying. In short, you don't need hair on your chest nor superhuman muscle development, just good training.

2 THE COMPLEAT TAILDRAGGER PILOT

GEOMETRY

Having successfully cleared away most of the smoke and some of the superstition, we can wrap up this section by stating that the difference between taildraggers and tricycle geared airplanes is nothing more than a *matter of geometry*. The geometry which we refer to is the placement of the landing gear with respect to the center of gravity.

In the next section we will look at this difference in geometry and assess how it will affect the airplane's sensitivity to the environment.

3

CONCEPTS AND THE ENVIRONMENT

Concepts are the tools which we use for problem understanding and solving, whereas the environment represents the framework within which the game must be played. The environment which the pilot operates in is the same whether he is flying a taildragger or tricycle gear. It is the same wind, and the airplane has the same torques applied (or does it?). At least on the surface this is how it appears. We've already discussed geometry a bit in the previous section, and we will soon see how the taildragger reacts differently to the environment than does the tricycle geared airplane. But before we look at this, we need to discuss a very important concept which we will then carry with us through this book like a security blanket. This is the notion of stability.

STABILITY

The concept of stability plays a very important part in the understanding of the control of a taildragger since it is this phenomena which makes the taildragger different from tricycle gear in terms of handling.

3 THE COMPLEAT TAILDRAGGER PILOT

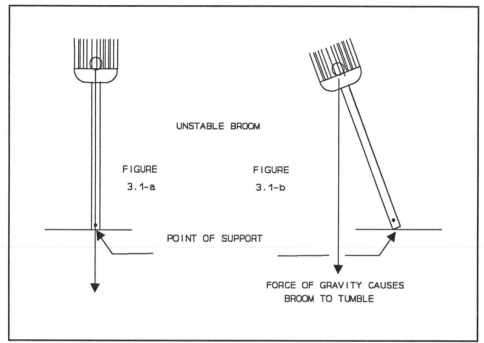

UNSTABLE BROOM

FIGURE
3.1-a

FIGURE
3.1-b

POINT OF SUPPORT

FORCE OF GRAVITY CAUSES
BROOM TO TUMBLE

Figure 3.1 Example of unstable object

Perhaps the simplest example of stability and instability is the broom balancing act. Imagine that you are trying to balance a broom which is inverted and has the tip of the handle resting in the palm of your hand (see Figure 3.1a). The force of gravity wants to make the broom fall and only some fairly fast and well coordinated reactions on your part will keep it from falling.

In Figure 3.1a, the broom stays at rest only as long as the line along which gravity is acting stays precisely in the center of the broom and passes through the point of support. As soon as the broom exhibits the slightest deviation from vertical, the gravitational force will no longer pass through the support point, and the result is a tendency to increase the displacement away from vertical as seen in Figure 3.1b. Ultimately, the broom will fall. This is why we call it unstable. A slight displacement away from center causes a rapid divergence following which it quickly becomes uncontrollable.

If you were to find and observe someone who is expert at this balancing act, you would soon notice that the balancing appears easy. Then, if you were to attempt it, would find it much more difficult than it appeared. You would probably find yourself chasing large excursions with what would soon seem to be an enormous amount of energy. This is precisely the situation facing the taildragger pilot at the instant of touchdown with any sideways drift. Both the broom and taildragger are unstable at this point.

On the other hand, Figure 3.2a shows a broom at rest in the pendulous position, and if we deflect it from the vertical by any reasonable amount, the force of gravity acts in a restorative direction and tends to reduce the displacement. We categorize this situation as stable. This is analogous to a tricycle geared airplane at the moment of touchdown. Both the broom and airplane are stable.

If you accept this analogy, there should be no doubt left in your mind as to which landing gear configuration requires the most skill in handling.

At this stage, most of the concepts to be discussed can best be explained by diagrams, hence we introduce the stick airplane shown

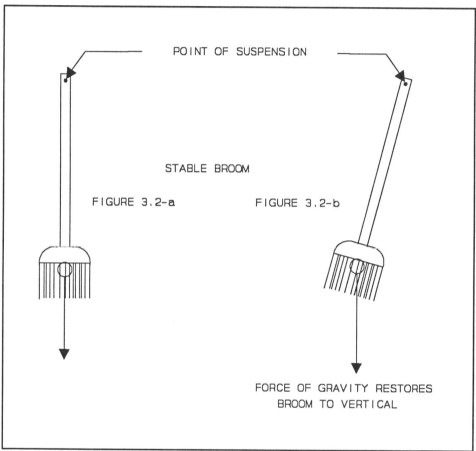

POINT OF SUSPENSION

STABLE BROOM

FIGURE 3.2-a   FIGURE 3.2-b

FORCE OF GRAVITY RESTORES
BROOM TO VERTICAL

Figure 3.2 Example of stable object

in Figures 3.3a and b. Note the difference between the geometry of the conventional geared airplane and the tricycle geared version. This is amplified in Figures 3.4 and 3.5 with all the other distracting items removed.

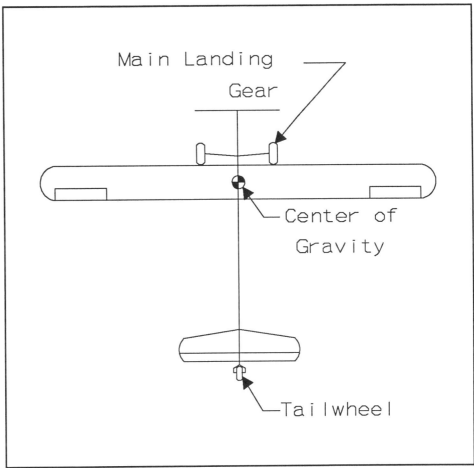

Figure 3.3a Taildragger diagram to be used for many of the explanations in this book

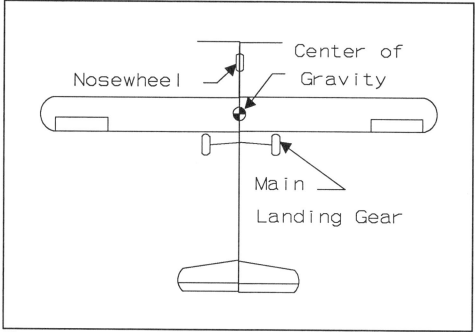

Figure 3.3b Tricycle geared airplane diagram

MOMENTUM

In order to discuss the subject intelligently, we need to introduce another important item, and that is momentum. Mathematically, momentum is the product of mass and velocity. However, for our purposes, we can assume that the weight of the airplane is going to remain constant during a landing (unless we land so hard that parts fall off) and consider that momentum, for a given airplane, will simply be proportional to velocity. This means that momentum has magnitude and direction, with the direction being the same as that of the velocity.

In other words, if the airplane is moving forward, it has forward momentum. On the other hand, if the airplane is moving forward and slightly to the side as in a slight crab, it has momentum forward and to the side.

In order to see how the two airplanes fit our concept of stability at touchdown, let's begin with a look at the tricycle geared airplane as it contacts the runway with a slight sideways drift.

Conditions:

1. Airplane is on a flight path parallel with the runway center line in a left crab (with a slight drift to the right).

2. Wind is from the left.

3. Airplane contacts ground with main gear.

For this part of the discussion, we are interested in the time interval beginning with contact of the main gear with the runway, until the nose wheel touches down. Let's look at the airplane in Figure 3.4a while remembering that the airplane has momentum to the right (perpendicular to the longitudinal axis) at the moment of touchdown. This comes from condition No. 1 above stating that drift to the right is present.

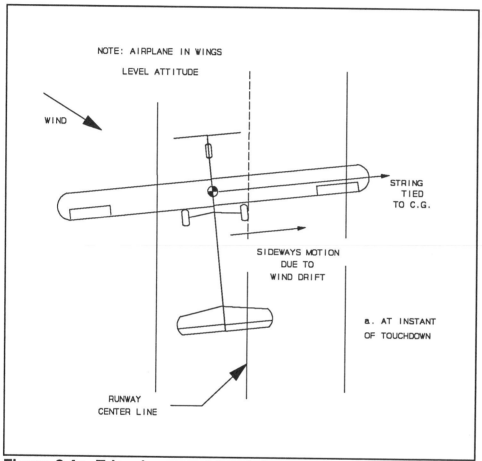

Figure 3.4a Tricycle gear at touchdown with drift

Imagine that this airplane in Figures 3.4a and b is a small balsa model and that a string is attached to the C.G. In order to determine what the momentum reaction of the airplane will be at the point of

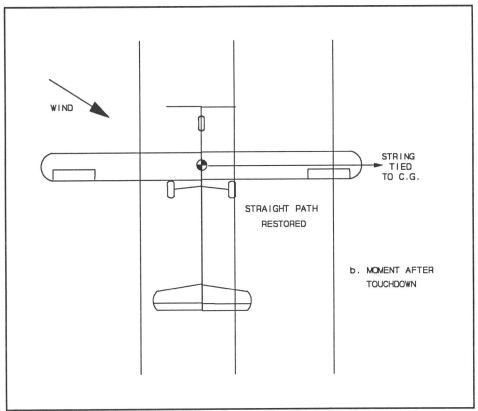

Figure 3.4b Tricycle gear after touchdown with drift

touchdown, we merely restrain the main gear with the fingers of the left hand and pull the string with the right hand in the same direction that the C.G. was moving in at the moment of touchdown. In other words, we pull to the right (in the direction of the momentum to the side, due to drift). The result is that the airplane wants to rotate clockwise or to the right, pivoting about the main gear.

3 THE COMPLEAT TAILDRAGGER PILOT

Note that the effect of the momentum is opposite to the weathervaning tendency of the airplane. Hence, the two tendencies oppose each other, with the landing gear geometry having created a stabilizing effect.

If we compare this reaction with that of the typical taildragger, we find that the difference is dramatic.

Conditions:

1. Airplane is on a flight path parallel with the runway center line in a left crab (with a slight drift to the right).

2. Wind is from the left.

3. Airplane contacts ground with main gear and unrestrained tailwheel.

In Figure 3.5a we are looking at the moment of impact, and in Figure 3.5b, the moment immediately after impact. Note that the sideward momentum, just like the pulling of the string, makes the airplane want to immediately swap ends, turning to the left. This desire is not only dramatic, it is catastrophic and is the genesis of the classic ground loop. The rotation to the left will be further compounded by the weathervaning effect of the wind from the left striking the tail. Thus, the combination of the weathervaning and drift forces add in the undesired direction, and the gear geometry can be said to have provided a de-stabilizing effect. In the case of tricycle gear, these two forces are in opposite directions thereby having a significant canceling effect.

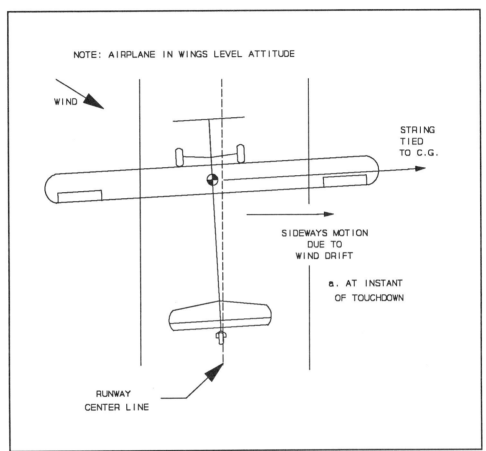

NOTE: AIRPLANE IN WINGS LEVEL ATTITUDE

WIND

STRING
TIED
TO C.G.

SIDEWAYS MOTION
DUE TO
WIND DRIFT

a. AT INSTANT
OF TOUCHDOWN

RUNWAY
CENTER LINE

Figure 3.5a Taildragger at touchdown with drift

If we were to compare the airplanes of Figures 3.4 and 3.5 with the brooms in Figure 3.1 and 3.2, we would find that the airplane momentum in the direction of the drift acts exactly like the force of gravity in the broom analogy. In the case of the stable broom or

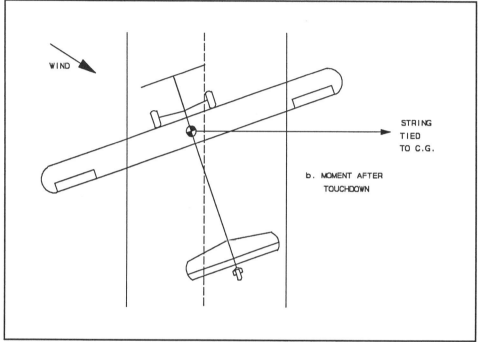

WIND

STRING
TIED
TO C.G.

b. MOMENT AFTER
   TOUCHDOWN

Figure 3.5b Taildragger after touchdown with drift

tricycle geared airplane, the force of gravity or the sideways
momentum acts to decrease the deflection from the desired direction.
On the other hand, the momentum resulting from drift tends to pull
the taildragger away from the center line like the gravity force tends
to displace the inverted broom. It also follows, although it certainly
is not obvious at this point, that where the inverted broom can be
more easily balanced if the balancer is quick and never lets the
deflections from the vertical get large, the same applies to the
taildragger pilot. If the deflections in direction are small, they may

be quickly corrected by the control available. Likewise, small deflections ignored will quickly get out of hand and become large enough that full control application (including full brake) will be insufficient to remedy the situation.

Note that this short discussion has not been meant as a complete discussion of how to land a taildragger. Rather it is intended to drive home the simple concept of stability and to demonstrate how the two types of airplane differ in this respect.

The more complete discussion will be covered in a later chapter where such items as the weathervaning tendency and influence of nose wheel or tailwheel / tail-skid will be discussed and added to further complicate the picture.

At this moment it is sufficient that you are now convinced that the analogy of the broom balancing act for the taildragger pilot is not that large an exaggeration.

Before we proceed to the handling of the airplane, let's examine the external factors acting on the airplane. Once we understand them and their effects, we will have a much better idea of how to cope with the problems created by the combination of environment and airplane.

THE ENVIRONMENT

These four most important components of the environment are the following:

1. Torque
2. Wind
3. Runway Surface
4. Airplane Characteristics

Each of the above factors deserves a detailed discussion because, while they have been explained in many textbooks, these explanations don't always give adequate perspective from the taildragger pilot's viewpoint. Secondly, they are to some extent ignored by many pilots (mostly tricycle gear pilots to be sure) without said pilots having come to grief. Hence, many have developed bad habits which they must drop, for these same habits practiced in a taildragger will bring sudden grief in copious amounts. Finally, until these factors and their effects are thoroughly understood, there is little point in discussing takeoff and landing techniques.

TORQUE

Much has been said about torque and how it affects airplanes. Many of the purists will complain that what we generally call torque is not really torque. So be it. The fact is that the word "torque" has such accepted usage that any attempt to change it and introduce new terminology would be ridiculous. Our basic objective is to develop an understanding of the various components of torque and how they change as a function of airplane conditions, i.e. throttle setting, attitude, and speed. A second objective is to explore what many of the other books have ignored which is the question "what is the difference between how the torque components affect a taildragger versus a tricycle geared airplane?" We will reserve for a later chapter a graphic description of how the various components of torque change as we follow the airplane through the takeoff run.

The latter is particularly important since without it, we cannot logically explain the apoplectic gyrations of the rudder pedals which the taildragger pilot engages in during every normal takeoff.

Torque is made up of at least four significant components which are not necessarily all present at the same time nor in all aircraft types.

1. Rotating Slipstream

As long as the propeller rotates, the slipstream which it forces to the rear will also rotate with a slight corkscrew motion. However, because most aircraft have an unbalanced vertical fin and rudder area, (most of the vertical fin is above the aircraft's longitudinal center line) the rotating slipstream strikes the left side of the vertical fin and rudder exerting a force that turns the airplane to the left. This is the most important torque component since it affects all aircraft, even in steady cruise flight.

There are several means which can be used to offset this left turning tendency, such as:

A. Offsetting the vertical fin slightly to the left. This would give nearly the same effect as a slight amount of right rudder.

B. Canting the engine thrust line slightly to the right.

C. Adding a ground adjustable trim tab to the rudder and adjusting it to provide the correct amount of right rudder in cruise flight.

D. Designing an airplane with balanced rudder and vertical fin areas (areas below the longitudinal center line equal to the area above the center line).

Various manufacturers have used A through C above either singly or in combination to solve this problem. I don't know of any contemporary general aviation airplane which uses D.

The sum total of all this as it affects you, the pilot, is that the left turning tendency has been neutralized during cruise flight. At speeds below cruise, such as during climb, the left turning tendency is not fully compensated and the pilot must hold right rudder to obtain a straight climb. Conversely, during a glide with reduced power, the slipstream effect is reduced although the manufacturer's compensation is still present. Hence the left turning tendency has been over-compensated and a slight amount of left rudder is needed for a straight descent. The exact amount will vary with engine power and descent air speed.

2. Opposite Reaction to Propeller Rotation

As long as the propeller rotates under power, the fixed part of the engine—the crankcase—will apply the same force to the airframe that the crankshaft applies to the propeller. This gives the airframe a tendency to rotate about its longitudinal axis in the direction opposite that of the propeller. If no compensation were built in for this, the airplane would fly in a constant slow roll. Of course, since the airframe is of high mass and high moment of inertia due to long wings, it would rotate much slower than the propeller.

This tendency to rotate is corrected for by the manufacturer by increasing the angle of incidence of the left wing. This gives the left wing a shade more lift than the right one and prevents the airplane from constantly rolling to the left. This, however, does not come without a price. The increased angle of incidence means that the left wing will always have a higher angle of attack than the right wing resulting in increased induced drag for the left wing. This higher drag in the left wing causes a left turning tendency which is compensated for in the same manner as the rotating slipstream. Note that here again the compensation built into the airplane is only correct for one set of conditions—usually cruising.

3. Asymmetric Loading of the Propeller

This phenomenon, commonly called P-Factor, normally is present anytime the engine is developing power and the aircraft is not going in the direction in which it is pointed. Provided of course, that the airplane has some forward speed. For example, there is no P-Factor when the airplane is held by brakes or chocks even though the engine may be revving up to full power and the propeller is at a normal pitch setting. The reason is that the airplane in that situation has no forward speed. A good example of when asymmetric propeller loading exists is shown by our stick airplane in slow flight as depicted in Figure 3.6. Note that the airplane is moving in a horizontal line while the longitudinal axis of the airplane is pointing 27 degrees above the horizon. This results in the propeller plane of

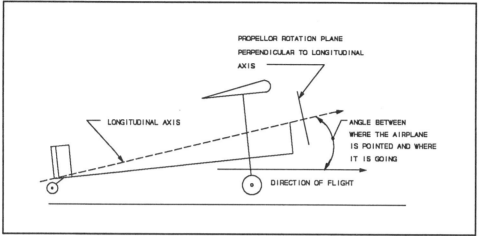

Figure 3.6 Typical airplane attitude in slow flight (or during initial take-off roll)

rotation being tilted 27 degrees from the line of forward velocity.

The P-Factor is developed by the fact that the downward moving blade (blade on the right-hand side of the airplane) has a higher angle of attack than the upward moving blade on the opposite side of the airplane. In addition, the downward blade also has slightly higher relative velocity with respect to the air. From the general theory of aerodynamics we know that higher speed and higher angle of attack both result in more lift—or in this case—thrust. Hence the blade on the right develops more thrust than that on the left with the final result being that the airplane wants to turn to the left. Since this is only a temporary condition present during the takeoff roll (that portion during which the tail is still down), climbs, and slow flight, the manufacturer makes no attempt at compensating for this and the pilot is required to compensate with a heavy right foot or rudder trim if the airplane is so equipped.

Most pilots are forced to accept the above description of P-Factor on faith simply because the training manuals don't normally treat the subject in greater depth. In our case however, a specific example is presented in detail in Appendix B for the person with interest in following through in order to satisfy his or her curiosity.

4. Gyroscopic Precession

The propeller spinning at an appreciable speed also acts like a giant sized gyro. Therefore, in order to determine what strange forces the prop may exert on the airplane in flight we must resort to the mathematics of the gyrodynamic world. And, because we have no desire to get bogged down in the math, let's simplify the problem down to one important equation given as:

$$T = \omega \; x \; H \qquad (3\text{-}1)$$

where T is the torque required to change the plane of rotation about the vertical axis, ω is the rate at which we are changing the plane of rotation about the horizontal axis, and H is the angular momentum of the prop.

What all this means is that as long as the airplane remains in a constant attitude, the propeller (gyro) is spinning in a given plane and ω is zero. The resulting torque, T, is then also zero. However, as soon as we attempt to change the airplane's attitude—such as rotating from cruise to climb—we force the prop to rotate in a different plane. While the propeller is changing planes of rotation, it exerts a force or torque on the airplane of a magnitude given by the previous equation. This force results in a tendency to turn left when the nose is lowered, or turn right when the nose is raised. The important point to note is that this force is proportional to the speed with which the propeller is forced to change planes of rotation. This is ω in equation 3-1. And, by the same token, it is only present while the attitude change is in process. This is what makes life exciting for the tyro taildragger pilot.

The relative magnitude of the different torque components will vary considerably between airplane types. While they all tend to be proportional to horsepower, airplane design also comes into the equation. Also, another item varying a great deal between successive airplane types is the ability to control this torque, and this very characteristic may affect a pilot's perception of torque. These can be rudder displacement, effectiveness, as well as brake effectiveness. Let's look at an example in order to get the point across. Assume that two airplanes are of equal weight, and have identical engines and propellers. Then let's describe airplane "A" as being low wing with wide landing gear spread, while airplane "B" is of high wing design, and has a rather small rudder displacement. On the takeoff run, both airplanes will have nearly identical torque values, but guess which one will acquire the reputation for having high torque and being a squirrel. This will be airplane "B" of course, primarily because of lower rudder effectiveness, lower brake effectiveness in steering (due to the narrower gear tread), and higher C.G. (due to the high wing design). Hence, what the pilot perceives as high torque is in fact greater difficulty in controlling the torque. In any case, one of the habits which each pilot should develop and which can go a long way in helping to control the torque equally well in large or small airplanes is gentleness in advancing the throttle and in raising the tail. Some of the reasons for this will be seen in Chapter 5.

The preceding will suffice as an explanation of torque at this stage, whereas the impact of torque and how it is controlled will be treated where it causes the greatest aggravation for the pilot, and that is in the chapter on takeoffs.

WIND

The second important factor to be studied is Wind. Except on the calmest day--which probably exists so seldom that most of us will see this no more than once or twice a year--the wind blows in varying degree and direction and is an environmental factor which all pilots must contend with. Here, is the most significant dividing line between tricycle gear and taildragger pilots.

The average pilot's (tri-gear of course) appraisal of the wind before flight consists of a brief glance at the wind sock, strictly for the purpose of making a go-no go decision and/or to see which runway may be in use. He is then likely to taxi out for takeoff without another look at the wind indicator. This isn't intended as a constant maligning of tricycle gear pilots. It is simply an attempt at indicating the bad habits which have been acquired along the way, and in this case habits encouraged by the fact that the typical tricycle geared airplane is of extremely stout construction and very forgiving of these habits.

3   THE COMPLEAT TAILDRAGGER PILOT

To the taildragger pilot, wind is a constant challenge, against which he will repeatedly test his skills, honing them to razor sharpness. Wind is a factor to be constantly measured, sensed, assessed, guessed at, cursed and overcome. In the right proportions, it can turn what initially was a pleasant day into an exciting challenge.

An average pilot taxiing out for takeoff may not be particularly bothered by the fact that two wind socks in different areas of the field may be blowing in different directions. Indeed, he might not even notice that there are two wind socks or that they don't agree. To the taildragger pilot, the difference is another factor to be assessed in relation to how it will affect his departure and is information to be salted away until the moment of need. He will note that conflicting wind sock indications in a relatively small geographical area i.e. that of an airport generally means that some form of wind shear activity is present, and will prepare himself accordingly. It is an incompetent pilot who doesn't learn from the available indications and is then suddenly surprised to find out--on short final--that there is wind shear present.

In fact, one of the great difficulties in transitioning pilots to taildraggers today is this lack of regard they have for the wind. Consequently, they continuously beat the hell out of the tricycle gear they normally fly. The fact that we don't have more bent landing gear accidents is a tribute to the gear's strength, not to the pilot's skills.

It has been my experience (as a general aviation check pilot for over eighteen years) that, while many of the general aviation pilots have the necessary crosswind skills, many are sadly lacking in the judgment that tells them "when" to apply those skills. A good example of this is the typical check ride (could be a Biennial Flight Review) during which the pilot makes a number of landings without the least attempt at a crosswind correction even though the crosswind component may be 5 to 10 knots. Yet, as soon as the instructor or examiner says "let's have a crosswind landing next", the crosswind correction is beautifully cranked in and a perfect landing ensues. What was the missing ingredient in the previous landings? You've got it, judgment. The skill was there in sufficient magnitude, and was available, but the judgment was lacking.

This experience tells me that today's students are well taught how to make crosswind takeoffs and landings, but are not taught when! I submit that many of the crosswind accidents happening today occur because the pilot took no notice of all the available wind cues and didn't realize that a correction was necessary until the wind had raised the wing tip at least 2 feet. By this time, a frantic correction is usually an exercise in futility.

A second source of wind induced taildragger landing accidents is the down-wind landing. In today's flight environment, the sensitivity of the taildragger to down-wind operations (takeoffs and landings) is either forgotten or in some cases was never known. Tower and Flight Service Station personnel are often quite ignorant of this factor and insist on using the down-wind runway for various reasons such as noise abatement. The tricycle geared airplane can handle this without a problem, but to the taildragger, a demon is lurking. The experienced taildragger pilot will, in this situation, request use of the upwind runway.

To summarize, the taildragger pilot must be super conscious of the wind and of it's effect on his aircraft. Very often, the wind will constitute his most serious limitation. It is important to bear in mind that this limitation is one which can be overcome to some extent as the pilot learns and develops the proper skills.

RUNWAY

To many pilots, a runway is a runway without need for further distinction. The type of runway surface may not seem important, with most pilots having a decided preference for the hard surface kind. Yet, the runway characteristics which we generally ignore can on occasion be extremely important to the taildragger pilot, especially on those occasions when the deck seems to have been stacked against him. While it is dangerous to generalize, we can point out factors concerning the runway which are very often true and can be crucial.

For example, paved runways at the smaller airports are generally narrow or are at least narrower than the grass runway would have been if it hadn't been paved. The paved runway also generally has edge obstructions such as runway lights. These can also be accompanied by height differences between the paved and unpaved portions of the landscape, and let's not forget the presence of the perennial ditch parallel to the paved runway. All of these factors preclude the possibility of landing in any direction other than perfectly aligned with the runway. Also, the lack of "give" which the paved surface has cannot be counted upon to help the pilot touching down with a slight drift. Given the availability of a grass field, the pilot may be able to land at some angle with the runway heading, thereby significantly reducing the crosswind component. He might also be able to capitalize on the grass's slipperiness, especially if it is wet. The experienced taildragger pilot may well do these things subconsciously. The above stated features of grass runways are all on the plus side.

Still, there can be some negative points to operations on grass. The presence of chuck holes, gradients, and hummocks can be detrimental to safe flight. The latter may increase the difficulty level of a wheel landing at a time when it is needed most.

When available for training operations, a good grass field is a definite advantage. Of course, any recommendation of grass fields should be accompanied by the warning that the grass field be personally checked out by the instructor before it is used for training. Even if it is a registered airport, the instructor's knowledge of the location of soft spots after a rainy day as well as of broken fence posts lying off to the side may well prevent an accident some day.

AIRPLANE CHARACTERISTICS

Finally, if we are to do justice to this discussion, we must list and examine those characteristics which separate one airplane model from another—at least insofar as they are important to the taildragger driver.

The first of course is torque, but considering its importance, it deserved its own place and has already been discussed extensively.

3 THE COMPLEAT TAILDRAGGER PILOT

Next is landing gear geometry which includes gear tread (spacing between the two main wheels), distance between main gear and tail wheel, and relationship of all these to the center of gravity.

Taildraggers with narrow gear tread are more difficult to steer in the face of crosswinds and other disturbances than those with wider gear. Likewise, those with high C. G. are also more difficult to cope with. Next are factors such as type of shock strut on the main gear. The main gear on a Piper J-3, an Aeronca 7AC, and a Cessna 140 are all different and accordingly, they behave differently. I'm not about to suggest which one is better, but different they are!

Also on the list are the many variations in tail gear. We have antiques still sporting tail skids, then we have full swivel non steerable tail wheels, and tail wheels which are steerable for the first 25 degrees of deflection and which become full swivel beyond that range. In addition, there are such devices as tail wheels that are steerable when the stick is held back and become full swivel when the stick is allowed to go forward (the P-51 Mustang and some versions of the North American T-6 are so equipped), and finally there are those aircraft with tail wheels which can be locked for the takeoff and landing runs. Among these are the Waco UPF-7, the DC-3, and some versions of the Harvard (Canadian T-6). Likewise are the Cessna 185's and the late model 180's. The purpose of this discussion is to alert the taildragger pilot to all of the above possibilities, and to urge him to completely familiarize himself with the airplane Owner's Manual or flight handbook before he discovers the differences the hard way. As an example, the North American T-6 can be found in configurations with the full swivel (unsteerable), the steerable type which automatically transitions to full swivel when the steerable range is exceeded, and the type which is steerable when the stick is held full to the rear. You can well imagine the confusion which would be felt by a pilot used to flying the model with steerable tail wheel, who one day climbs into a friend's SNJ (Navy version of the T-6) without having familiarized himself with the Handbook, only to find out on a narrow taxi-way that this airplane's tail wheel is fully castering and nonsteerable. If it is a gusty winter day and the taxi-way is lined with snow banks which have turned solid, the price paid for the pilot's carelessness may be a new elevator. So heed the warnings, and study the handbooks carefully.

These differences, as important as they may be, are all somewhat obvious, but there are more subtle differences however which can be as important. These range from quality and usefulness of the brakes, rudder effectiveness, and size of the vertical fin. Two aircraft noted for poor brake systems as well as limited rudder are the Bellanca Cruisair series and the Globe / Temco Swift. While both are very desirable airplanes, and I would be proud to own either one, they cannot handle crosswind components that many other taildragger models will take in stride.

The size of the vertical fin determines the airplane's weathervaning tendency, with some like the Stinson Station Wagon and Republic Seabee having more than their fair share of either. Of course, it is possible to find airplanes which initially had poor handling records but have since been modified such as by the installation of larger or more positive acting brakes, etc., hence one must be extremely careful before maligning any particular breed.

In passing, let's not forget one other important option on a few taildraggers, and that is the Cross Wind landing gear. At least two different versions of the Goodyear Cross Wind gear and one by Geisse have been approved for mounting on several popular General Aviation taildraggers. In brief, the Cross Wind gear consists of main gear which are capable of castering individually within narrow limits in order to align themselves with the motion of the aircraft relative to the ground. In other words, if the airplane is in a sidewards drift at the moment of touchdown, the Cross Wind gear will caster allowing this motion rather than offering the resistance of the normally fixed main gear which would immediately initiate a ground loop.

The first of the two Goodyear versions is the unlocked type. This gear is always unlocked and can caster anytime the sideward castering forces exceed a pre-established spring detent force. The second type has locking pins allowing the crosswind castering feature to be locked out for taxiing purposes. This feature was added by Goodyear to provide a bit more controllability to the taxiing phase. While we will discuss these features in more detail later, suffice it to say that taxiing with the Cross Wind gear unlocked on a gusty day can lead to some exciting moments, especially if the taxiway is narrow and bordered by snow banks. There are other versions of Cross Wind gear in existence, but the two just mentioned represent the vast majority still in use. In the final analysis, you will probably find them on less than 2 percent of the taildraggers in existence and you will also find as many pilots opposed to their use as you find in favor of this item. Additional information on the use of Cross Wind gear is included in Chapter 8.

Angular Momentum

Angular momentum, which is dependent on the moment of inertia of an airplane, is an important and often ignored characteristic of a taildragger. Since this book is intended for pilots rather than for engineers, we will stick to a definition which can be readily understood by all, even if the purist would refuse to accept it.

Angular momentum is the property of a rotating body that makes it want to continue rotating. In this case, we are interested in the angular momentum of an airplane about its yaw axis. It is dependent on angular velocity and moment of inertia. The moment of inertia is in turn dependent on the mass and the distance of the mass from the axis of rotation. Without getting technical, you can see that an airplane with a longer engine or with an engine placed farther forward from the main gear than another will have a higher moment of inertia. If turned at the same rate, it will have a higher angular momentum.

What this means to you as a pilot is that an airplane with a big engine mounted way out front will present control difficulties on the ground in proportion to all this. It will require more rudder to initiate a turn, and likewise will require a larger and an earlier application of opposite rudder to straighten out the airplane at the completion of the turn.

This is perhaps epitomized by the Curtis P-40. When you look at a photograph of this airplane and see the long heavy engine so far forward, it is easy to visualize why the airplane was ground looped so easily and so often by the early World War II pilots transitioning into the type.

Visibility

Taildraggers in general tend to have a reputation for poor visibility. This is the first characteristic which will accost the beginner as soon as the individual sits in the airplane for the purpose of proceeding with taidragger training. The first reaction gives rise to the question "how does one <u>see</u> out of these things?" Here is significant difference between the taildragger and its tricycle geared brother. Still, it would be incorrect and a gross exaggeration to state that all taildraggers have poor visibility. Several of the more modern types, and this includes the Cessna series from 120 through the 185, the Aeronca's and their derivatives (Citabria and Decathlon), as well as the Luscombe and Taylorcraft have excellent visibility. The term excellent is used here in the sense that the airplane can be taxied without the pilot having to resort to S-turns.

And then, there are the others. Most of the older bi-planes as exemplified by the Stearman and Waco UPF-7 have little visibility straight ahead while in the three-point attitude, and visibility to the sides is somewhat impaired by the presence of the wings and struts. In these and similar airplanes, S-turns become an absolute require-ment if the airplane is to be taxied safely. Perhaps the best and closest example of poor visibility is the venerable J-3 Cub, when the front seat is occupied by a burly instructor and the taxiing is attempted by a petite student in the rear seat. This student will most likely taxi with the door open, and with the head and shoulders extended as far out to the right side of the airplane as possible regardless of the outside temperature. Any attempt to taxi without the use of S-turns in such a situation would be foolhardy in the extreme.

Because of the poor visibility and the need for S-turns, taildragger taxiing is usually performed at lower speeds.

Here we must add a note of caution for the beginner, and that is to point out the need for exercising constant vigilance concerning the location of the tail during the S-turns, especially if the taxiway is narrow.

Once the pilot gains a bit of experience in taxiing the taildragger, the visibility problem will gradually recede, and the taxiing will become relatively pleasant. However, the visibility problem will still persist to some degree for takeoffs and landings. In the case of the takeoff, visibility is a problem only until the tail is raised. Hence, the problem is of relatively short duration. But, in the case of landings, the agony of insufficient visibility begins with the turn to final and lasts until roll-out is complete. To be sure, there are some tricks which will help a bit, such as making no straight finals. If the turn to final is kept in a constant arc, the pilot has some visibility to the side (known in some quarters as an SCA, for *Spitfire Curved Approach*). Another partial solution is to use wheel landings a high percentage of the time, since, the view is better with the tail up than with it in three-point attitude. Nevertheless, while these stratagems provide some help, the problem is never entirely solved. Eternal vigilance is the price of admission to the taildragger fraternity.

3   THE COMPLEAT TAILDRAGGER PILOT

At this point, we've introduced all of the topics that pertain to the fast disappearing art of taildragger flying. If it has appeared dry, let's bear in mind that the individual ingredients of any soup are not very interesting. It is the combination which makes it all worthwhile. None of this is intended to scare you away from taildraggers, rather it is presented in order that you may approach the airplane fore-armed with knowledge.

GROUND OPERATIONS

In the previous chapter we've discussed almost all of the variables which will affect the pilot's performance. However, we have intentionally omitted one, and that is the pilot's skill. The remainder of this book is intended as an aid in developing just that.

ENGINE START

The first major difference in procedure which the tyro taildragger pilot will encounter when transitioning from tricycle-gear is the positioning of the controls at the moment of engine start.

In a tricycle geared airplane, the pilot often ignores the position of the control wheel while his hands are occupied with the starter, ignition switch and throttle. In the taildragger, even the smallest one, he must hold the stick (wheel) in the rearward position (with knees or elbows if necessary), while the hands are occupied with the starter, ignition, etc. The reason for this procedure is to prevent a nose-over in the remotely possible event that the engine should catch with a higher throttle setting than anticipated and with the stick forward. This could cause the tail to rise unexpectedly from the reaction of the lowered elevator to the high level of the slipstream resulting in the bending of propeller, cowling, pride, and bank account.

The tricycle gear pilot seldom worries about this, because the tail of his airplane is already up, and can hardly go higher, and the nose can hardly go lower[1] since it is firmly planted on a nose wheel.

The taildragger pilot who ignores this obviously important step will be looked at askance by his fellow pilots who will proceed to make book on when his first "surprise" will happen.

BEFORE TAXIING

Assuming that the proper checklist items have been completed, the final item is to check that both brakes are operating properly. While this step is also desired for any type of airplane, it is much more important for the taildragger because of the taildragger's ability to make sharp turns in tight quarters. This ability is a great advantage until you try taxiing—with a stuck brake—away from the gas pump and wipe out the gas pump with the horizontal stabilizer. A tricycle geared airplane under the same conditions would not be able to turn as fast, and might have been caught in time to avert the catastrophe. Yet, telling the FBO that "this couldn't have happened in a tri-gear" will be small consolation.

---

[1] With the possible exception of when in the presence of a high quartering tail wind.

TAXIING

Once the brakes have been tested and determined to be o.k., and the airplane is in motion, the tyro taildragger pilot must guard against his first bad habit as a tricycle gear pilot and that is taxiing at excessively high speeds. It is fair to say that most tri-gear pilots taxi much faster than they should. They find the airplane to be so controllable that they are easily lulled into a false sense of security, convinced that it can be controlled and stopped just like the family car.

The taildragger pilot must use only enough power to start the airplane moving, and then retard the throttle to achieve a speed no greater than a fast walk. To use more power than this may require excessive use of the brakes to slow the airplane with consequent overheating of the brakes. That this has happened may not be apparent until one overheated brake "grabs" during the takeoff run. This can be an exciting experience. More importantly, taxiing at excessive speed will aggravate the airplane's tendency to sway from side to side as the wheels hit small bumps. On a windy day, this swaying motion may allow a wing tip to rise just enough to allow the wind to get under that wing and start the process which could result in the ground being scraped by the opposite wing tip. As for use of the controls during taxiing, a certain pattern of use can make taxiing easier and safer and can make the difference between a rough day and a catastrophe when operating in high winds.

ELEVATORS

The elevators should be up, stick (yoke) back when taxiing upwind and positioned down, stick (yoke) forward, when taxiing downwind. The latter is the step usually forgotten. It is important however since a sudden gust of wind while taxiing downwind with the elevators up could very easily pick up the tail and result in a very quick conversion to a roto-tiller.

AILERONS

When taxiing crosswind, the stick (yoke) should be "into the wind". This will result in the windward aileron being deflected upwards and reduce the lift of the windward wing. If this is not done and the stick is held neutral while crosswind, the upwind wing will have more lift than the leeward wing due to dihedral (if present), and the wind direction. The result would be that the windward wing will tend to ride a bit higher than the other. This is a ground loop waiting to happen, and the next wind gust may just determine the time and place.

When taxiing upwind or downwind the ailerons are held in the neutral position until a turn is anticipated. At that time, aileron into the wind will be used to lead the turn, and the aileron will then be reversed as soon as the airplane passes the crosswind position. Is that clear? No? Well, we'll try it again more slowly.

Imagine that you are taxiing upwind and wish to make a 180 turn downwind. You obviously have the choice of turning left or right as in Figure 4.1. (We've added the ailerons to our "stick" airplane in

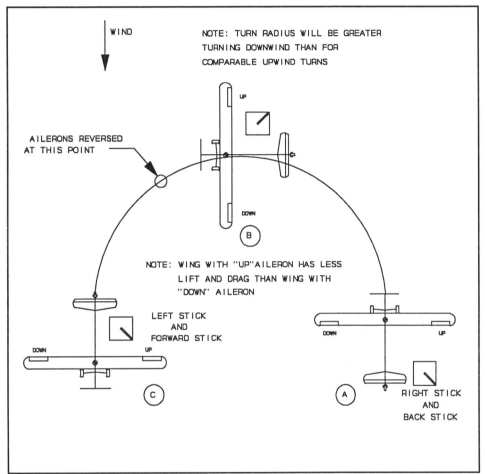

Figure 4.1 Use of ailerons in taxiing turn to <u>downwind</u>

order to help the explanation along.)

Briefly, note that the airplane at (A) will see a crosswind from the right when it reaches position (B). Hence, aileron into the wind, or right stick (wheel) will be needed at that point just as we've discussed under crosswind taxiing. The difference here is that right stick should be applied when the turn is initiated. This action, due to the increased drag of the down aileron, will aid the turn. However, as soon as the crosswind position is passed, the ailerons are reversed causing the following wind to apply more push to the right aileron than to the left, thereby again aiding the turn.

Run through this a couple more times and it will seem much simpler. You will also see why it is so important to keep track of wind direction on a continuous and practically subconscious basis.

For the sake of completeness, we show the opposite case, turning from downwind to upwind in Figure 4.2. [2]

Again, since the crosswind will be from the left when he reaches (B), the pilot leads with left stick from (A) until he has passed (B) at which point the ailerons are quickly reversed.

The use of ailerons in the above described manner is generally restricted to light or medium winds, and the greatest benefit of proper usage will be felt in airplanes without brakes or steerable tail wheel. These airplanes need all the help they can get to make them turn properly. However, in the presence of severe winds, aileron use

---

[2] Figures 4.1 and 4.2 are adapted from Reference 2 which remains the most useful volume in the author's library.

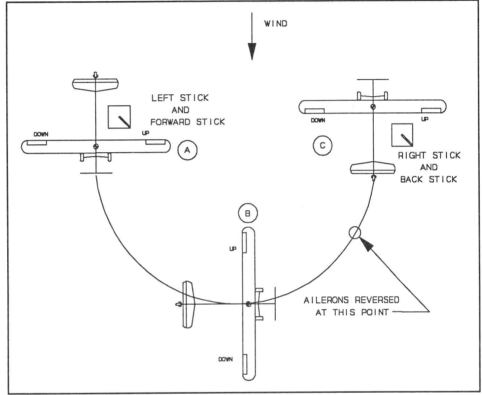

Figure 4.2 Use of ailerons in taxiing turn to <u>upwind</u>

should concentrate on holding the windward wing down and therefore may differ slightly from the diagrams shown.

If the taildragger in question is equipped with effective brakes and steerable tail wheel, the aforementioned finesse with the ailerons will not be required, although it is still important to hold the windward wing down in a crosswind. The reason for teaching this aileron usage is to prepare the taildragger pilot for future flight in antiques, many of which are without brakes. It will also help when the brake equipped airplane suffers a brake failure.

RUDDER

There is nothing complicated about rudder use in the turn. However, the previously mentioned factor of airplane angular momentum will obviously temper the amount of rudder used and its timing. Simply, the larger the airplane, the more rudder will be required to initiate the turn, and the sooner after the turn is initiated will opposite rudder need to be applied in order to stop the turn at the proper point. This will depend on the airplane of course. By comparison, when performing a 360° turn in the air, you may start reducing the bank angle towards recovery 15 to 30 degrees before the required heading. On the ground you will become accustomed to initiating a recovery 90 degrees or more before the desired heading, especially if the day is windy and the desired heading is not into the wind.

You will note after the first couple of tries that turning upwind is easy and can be accomplished with a surprisingly short radius of turn and with little application of rudder or brake. On the contrary, turning downwind can be downright tricky, and will be with a much wider radius at best. This is a point at which the difference between taildragger and tricycle gear is very much apparent. In the average tricycle-gear with steerable nose wheel, the turn radius is determined by nose wheel deflection and little else. And the pilot consequently does not need to take the difference in turn radii into account.

The discussion up to this point has been based on the assumption that the taildragger is of conventional type, that is to say is equipped with the following:

1. Straight gear (rather than Cross Wind gear)

2. A steerable tail wheel (rather than a tail skid, or a full swivel tail wheel of the non-steerable type).

The biggest problem in learning to turn the taildragger is over-control, usually arising from excessive brake use. As the pilot gains experience, he will learn to use the brake sooner and in lesser amounts. One day he will be proud to learn that he can do most taxiing without use of brakes.

But let's spend a few moments discussing the tail wheel. The type most common in the taildraggers left in circulation and in those few still in production is the steerable tail wheel which can be steered via the rudder pedals through a range of plus or minus 25 degrees or so of tail wheel deflection. If the tail wheel is deflected beyond that range, either by wind or by braking action, it will become full swivel, and can then turn through a full 360 degrees. When it has gone beyond the limits of the steering range, it becomes non-steerable. It can be returned to the steerable mode by the simple expedient (not quite so simple if in the presence of a gusting crosswind) of taxiing forward enough to bring the tail wheel back close to neutral. As the tail wheel changes from the steerable to full swivel, a slight noise may be heard coming from the tail. The amplitude of this sound will of course depend on the type of airplane. If this sound is heard when it is anticipated, it simply means that the airplane has switched from a mode when steering was fairly easy and responsive to a mode in which steering is not so easy, is much less responsive, and on occasion is nigh impossible. It might also mean that you will need to use the brakes.

On the other hand, if you hear the sound when you are not anticipating it, it could well be the goodbye sound. (Like it's your guardian angel just departing and saying "see you later" because you've just completed one fourth of a groundloop).

The important factors to bear in mind at this point are twofold. First, the tyro taildragger pilot should attempt to keep the turns wide enough so that the tail wheel remains in the steerable range. This is true for the first few hours, and should not be construed to mean that the tail wheel should never be operated full swivel. After all, the full swivel feature was designed for a very good purpose and was meant to be used when needed. However, there is no point in unnecessarily tempting the gods too early in the game. Secondly, the pilot should remember to re-center the tail wheel to return it to the steerable mode as soon as possible. For example, the cowboy who turns onto the runway for takeoff with the tail wheel in full swivel and doesn't center it before applying takeoff power is an accident waiting for a place to happen. He has deliberately handicapped himself by discarding his most valuable card, and the pot may well exceed any he has ever seen in a poker game.

Before leaving the subject of tail wheels, we should consider that the above statements apply when the tail wheel mechanism is in good maintenance and working properly. Unfortunately, there is no shortage of units which have not been maintained or have been abused such as by hours of training which has exposed them to an excessive number of hard landings. In any case, they are not likely to function properly. The tail wheel with a broken steering mechanism may not cause you an accident (if you are lucky) but will at least bring you some degree of embarrassment, and according to Murphy's law, this will be when there are a maximum number of spectators present. So, beware the bent, sticky or broken hardware.

BRAKES

The recommended use of brakes in taxiing can be summarized into some very simple rules:

1. Use only an amount that is absolutely necessary.

2. Don't use them abruptly.

3. Don't turn with one brake completely locked.

It is normal, in the early stages of taildragger training, for the pilot to use much more braking action than is required by the situation. This should not cause alarm since there are two good reasons why it consistently happens:

1. The pilot was spoiled and picked up the bad habit while flying tricycle gear.

2. He hasn't yet learned how much can be accomplished using rudder and tail wheel nor has he picked up the skill and confidence required to do it.

As he progresses in training, he will learn to maneuver with the rudder and will place less emphasis on the brakes and his goal will be to use them as little as possible. This in turn will make the brakes last longer, will prevent their overheating and the dangerous possibility that they might seize, and will conserve tires.

According to Murphy's Law, "if things can go wrong, they will". And according to one of his corollaries of the law "if things go wrong, they will do so at the worst possible time and place". If we apply this law to the use of brakes, it shows that brakes overheated by overuse during taxiing will not seize while taxiing. Of course not! They will seize during the takeoff run, and while it might not ruin your whole day, it will be a day that you will not soon forget—ranking alongside other important days in your life such as your wedding day, Bar Mitzvah, and father-in-law's retirement day. If you manage to keep it on the runway when this happens, it will be because the runway is wide, ergo the airport is large and busy, and you will be blocking the runway until you have the airplane towed off. On the other hand, if you don't manage to stay on the runway, it may well be because you are at a very small airport, and it is going to be one hell of a ride through the puckerbrush.

The main reason for not applying the brakes abruptly is that such a practice can be cause of a nose-over which is likely to be expensive. Propellers cost money. This will of course depend on the model of airplane as well as its particular loading configuration. Some airplanes have the C.G. so close to the main gear that a slight touch on the brakes can raise the tail a foot off the ground. In others, full braking can be used without worrying. But be careful. You may have gotten away with heavy braking yesterday because you had full tanks and a thousand pound payload with the C.G. well aft. Today, ferrying the airplane back empty and with only 5 gallons left in the front tank, the same amount of braking may cost you a new constant speed prop and a crankshaft run-out inspection.

Finally, turns should not be made with one wheel locked—especially on a hard surface—because of the terrible strain and possible damage which the tire will experience as a result of such an unprofessional form of abuse. It may look flashy, but turning in this manner is a poor way to treat the machinery. The wheel on the inside of the turn should always be allowed to rotate slightly even if it rolls ahead only a few inches.

As the pilot becomes a true taildragger driver, his interests will probably gravitate towards many of the older and even antique airplanes. And then will run into another very important reason for not overusing the brakes. In many of the old birds, the brakes are unreliable and in many cases ineffectual due to poor design. This means that they will overheat even sooner than normal. In other birds, the brakes are mechanical and may need adjustment after every other time they are used. Also, the brakes adjusted properly for a cold day may "grab" when an unseasonably warm day comes along. Likewise, the brakes which worked fine all summer may not hold when the first cold front of autumn comes through.

Another source of brake problems in the old birds may be the shortage of available brake parts for proper maintenance. Many an owner has had to resort to home-made parts because the manufacturer of the original brake went out of business some twenty five years or so ago. The hand made parts used may be better than original, but on the other hand, they might be only half as good.

The accomplished taildragger pilot who learns and practices proper brake usage will gain a side benefit as a result. He will definitely lose the bad habit of using heavy braking to make the first turnoff after landing. Nuff said.

THROTTLE

Here is one control which is available to the pilot and which is used in a very different manner in a taildragger than in a tricycle geared airplane.

The throttle is normally advanced to start the airplane rolling, usually a bit more power is needed than in tricycle gear because of the increased friction of the smaller tail wheel. By the same token, the throttle will be retarded more as soon as the airplane starts moving, due to the slower taxiing speed of the taildragger.

In addition to this normal throttle usage, the pilot will find the throttle to be a very useful addition to rudder and brakes for turning. In most tricycle geared airplanes, the turn radius is limited by the physical limits through which the nose wheel can be deflected. Any attempt to reduce the radius with bursts of throttle will be ineffective and will produce nothing more than excessive side loads on the nose wheel assembly and strut.

In the taildragger, the combination of full rudder, a burst of throttle, and enough forward stick to relieve the tail wheel of most of the weight it is normally carrying can produce an incredibly small turn radius. Of course, all of these inputs must be applied in the properly measured amounts and with an exact sense of timing. It should not be attempted by the beginner. On the other hand, it is a skill to be developed as the training and learning progresses.

A variation of this type of turn is to use enough power and forward stick to physically pick the tail off the ground during the turn. This obviously requires a sense of timing approaching that of two porcupines mating. (It is impossible to do it slowly hence must be with extreme care!)

While the reader may conclude that this is a dangerous and needless maneuver, I disagree and have included it through my firm belief that a pilot should learn to control his airplane through every conceivable corner of the performance envelope. Only in this way will he develop the skills so necessary to cope with the unexpected situation which may one day face him. This applies to ground as well as flight maneuvers.

In fact, he may find this type of maneuver very necessary should he ever fly a World War I type of antique sans brakes and with a super rigid tail skid. Likewise, it may be a useful emergency maneuver for the pilot who unintentionally lands long at a short field in an airplane with a locked tail wheel, and then attempts to turn to avoid ditch or fence without the presence of mind to first unlock the tail wheel. In this case, the pilot's first indication of a problem is that the airplane rolls straight as a die even though full rudder has been applied. At this point, forward elevator and a burst of throttle will turn the airplane more quickly than fumbling with a lever to unlock the tail wheel.

I would point out though that blasting the tail around with the throttle should be done with the courtesy which years ago was taught with the maneuver. It should not be performed if the prop blast will shower sand and debris into an open hangar, or onto spectators, or parked aircraft.

HIGH SPEED TAXIING

The taildragger maneuver called "high speed taxiing" is performed by taxiing at speeds sufficiently high that the tail can be kept raised as in a takeoff or a wheel landing. From this description it must be obvious to the reader that it is a ticklish maneuver to be accomplished with extreme care. When the taxiing pilot arrives at his destination or at a point where a turn is required, the airplane must be slowed and the tail must be lowered to the ground as in the completion of a wheel landing. A little bit of imagination immediately suggests that this is not for tight quarters nor for inexperienced pilots. Perhaps the most common error is in not leaving sufficient space for the airplane to slow sufficiently before an attempted turn or stop. A second error is that of not paying enough attention to the control of angle of attack. If the tail is allowed to drop slightly while the airplane is rolling at sufficient speed, the ensuing increase in angle of attack can cause the airplane to leave the ground in an unpremeditated takeoff. The look of surprise on the pilot's face on such an occasion tends to be priceless. Finally, the pilot must religiously guard from an upset by the wind if the high speed taxiing is engaged in during high or gusting winds.

The bottom line on high speed taxiing is that it has some uses, but that the inherent risks in the maneuver should discourage its use in close quarters and by inexperienced pilots. Training in high speed taxiing should not be attempted until the student has mastered wheel landings. And, the training should then be conducted in areas with plenty of open space. (See chapter 9 for additional comments on this subject).

SPECIAL EQUIPMENT

The presence of certain special equipment can change the picture slightly.

The lockable tail wheel is perhaps the most common item of special equipment found. The typical one is different from the more conventional tail wheel discussed previously in that it can be in either one of two modes. Fully locked, it cannot be deflected and the airplane will roll straight. Unlocked, it usually is full swivel and non-steerable. This is the type found in most multiengined taildraggers such as the DC-3. Its non-steerable aspect is no great handicap since the airplane can easily be steered using the large brakes and differential power. In single engine airplanes, this feature is a bit more challenging since differential engine power is not available. In this case, the downwind 90 degree turn may have to be made in the form of a 270 degree upwind turn if the wind is strong. And the seasoned pilot will leave himself sufficient room to execute it.

In either case, the lockable tail wheel is normally locked for long stretches of straight taxiing—especially crosswind—and for all takeoffs and landings. Because it is not an item present in all taildraggers, its use should definitely be a "check list" item.

One exception to the lockable tail wheel type mentioned above is that found on Cessna 185's which is lockable for takeoffs and landings, and is steerable through a limited range when unlocked. It is full swivel when the steerable range is exceeded. This is the best of all taildragger worlds.

In an unfortunate accident involving a DC-3 some years ago, the takeoff was made by a pilot who was not type rated in the DC-3. Somehow, both front seat occupants neglected to lock the tail wheel, and what should have been a normal takeoff suddenly developed into a catastrophe with the airplane coming to rest in a ditch off the runway. The force of impact was strong enough to tear one engine from its mountings. So you see why it should be (and probably was) a check list item.

A second item of special equipment which one may encounter is the Cross Wind gear. In the case of the lockable Cross Wind gear, taxiing is exactly as with straight gear as long as one doesn't forget to lock the gear at the end of the landing run and straighten out the gear by use of the rudder if the gear was kicked out of detent by a crosswind landing.

On the other hand, if the Cross Wind gear is not locked or is of the non-lockable type, taxiing in strong crosswinds will become an exciting experience and add to the taildragger pilot's already busy life. In this day when everyone is talking about job enrichment, this is one guy who won't need or desire any further job enrichment. The truth of the matter is that taxiing the airplane in one direction while the nose is pointing in another takes a bit of getting used to. And the first attempts at it are akin to your first try at putting lots of English on a cue ball. Unless you use a lot of chalk, you're likely to miscue. I am firmly convinced, although I have never seen it in print, that the steering geometry of the Cross Wind gear has some unstable aspects to it. This may well be why this gear, which sometimes appears to be a godsend, has been cursed by so many pilots.

The Cross Wind gear is an important enough subject to deserve an entire chapter devoted to its use, and to the problems peculiar to its steering geometry (see Chapter 8).

5

TAKEOFF'S

It is this maneuver which comes as the biggest surprise to beginning taildragger pilots and causes them untold grief. In general most pilots converting to the tail wheel have heard all the wild tales concerning the difficulties in landing, and therefore approach it with the full expectation of trouble. Sooner or later, they are agreeably surprised to learn that the landing was not the "bête noire" which it was purported to be. On the other hand, no one has ever mentioned to them the various problems they will encounter during the takeoff and they approach it with the idea that it is similar to a tricycle gear takeoff except that a couple of steps need to be interchanged. In fact, if they had asked an instructor about the procedure used for the takeoff, they would most probably have been told to "open up the throttle, pick the tail up as soon as you can and let her fly herself off". Such an answer would have been a gross understatement, hence, the surprise when they try it.

In truth, practically all of the problems occurring during the takeoff are associated with torque. This is the reason for the long winded discussion of torque in an earlier chapter and why we will give it further treatment in this chapter. Once the reasons behind torque variations are understood, it becomes a simple matter to program the right foot to provide the proper compensation.

5 THE COMPLEAT TAILDRAGGER PILOT

NORMAL TAKEOFF

The normal takeoff is the basic maneuver from which all the other takeoffs are derived. It consists of the following phases or steps usually in the order presented:

1. Advancing the throttle and initial takeoff roll with tail wheel on the ground.

2. Lifting of the tail.

3. Takeoff roll with tail raised.

4. Fly-off.

In actual practice these four phases will be so blended together that there may be no obvious demarcation between one and the other. We do discuss it in four phases however because of the way in which it will be keyed in with our torque diagrams.

STEP 1. Advancing Throttle and Initial Takeoff Roll

The throttle is advanced from idle to full throttle in one gradual but positively continuous motion as would be done in a tricycle geared airplane. Naturally, the rate of throttle advance should not be so high as to damage the engine, especially if it is the supercharged engine of the larger taildragger.[1] In most light airplanes, the throttle will have reached the wide open position slightly before the tail is ready to be raised. During the initial takeoff roll, the airplane will typically surge to the left if left to its own devices, and will require much more rudder deflection to keep it rolling straight than a tricycle gear would.

And this is for the following two reasons:

1. The taildragger evidences more torque in this phase than the tricycle gear.

2. The tail wheel is farther away from the main gear than the nose wheel is in the tricycle gear, and is therefore less effective than a nose wheel as a steering device.

The taildragger has more torque than the tricycle gear because it is in a three point attitude (tail wheel on the ground) and the propeller plane of rotation is not perpendicular to the direction of motion. Instead, it is tipped slightly—usually about 10 degrees or so, hence the propeller is asymmetrically loaded. (Refer to the discussion of P-Factor in Chapter 3 and Figure 3.5. Also see Appendix B for a mathematical or vector development for specific examples). This results in torque that is usually absent in the tricycle gear because

---

[1] For example, the DeHavilland DHC-2 Beaver is powered by a Pratt and Whitney R-985 engine with an integral gear driven supercharger. The gear ratio is 10:1, and acceleration of the engine to 2400 RPM means that the supercharger has accelerated to 24,000 RPM in the same length of time. Hence, an excessively rapid acceleration of the engine can cause the supercharger drive shaft to shear.

it performs this portion of its takeoff roll with tail raised in a near level flight attitude.

STEP 2. Lifting of the Tail

The moment when the tail is lifted could easily be called "Torques in Transition". The torque due to P-Factor will decrease to zero since the airplane now approaches a level flight attitude. On the other hand, torque due to gyroscopic precession of the propeller will come in only during the act of lifting the tail and will then disappear. It will reach an intensity proportional to how quickly the tail is raised. It is therefore to the advantage of the beginner to raise the tail slowly, thereby creating a level of torque which can easily be controlled. The pilot can always experiment with raising the tail more quickly later when he has more experience and a better handle on the amount of control needed as compared with what is available. It is indeed possible to raise the tail so quickly (at a slow airspeed) that the pilot will run out of available rudder with the airplane veering off to the left while the right rudder pedal is firewalled. The proper rate of raising the tail will be demonstrated by your instructor. It is one of the points which cannot be learned from a book.

STEP 3. Takeoff Roll with the Tail Raised

This is often the step most feared by the beginner and unnecessarily so. The two problems which he is likely to visualize are the following:

1. The airplane must be terribly difficult to control while only on two wheels.

2. The bird must be prone to nosing over at the slightest hiccup.

The correct answer to both of these concerns is "none of the above", and for some good reasons. If the pilot has successfully controlled the airplane up to this point, he is unlikely to lose control now because at this speed the airplane is much more controllable than it was at lower speeds. This due to the increased air flow past the tail which increases the rudder's effectiveness tremendously. Likewise, the attitude of the airplane is quite controllable with the elevator, and will not be a problem as soon as the pilot understands what attitude to set up and which visual cues to use in order to accomplish this. One cue which is not to be used for this is the attitude gyro. The pilot's vision must be directed outside the cockpit.

STEP 4. Fly-off

This is the easiest step of all. Just a slight amount of back elevator to increase the angle of attack, and lift will accomplish the rest. As the tail is lowered for this, some P-Factor will re-enter the equation, but it generally will be inconsequential and will be easily compensated for by holding the slight amount of right rudder which any airplane needs during a climb.

While everything said above is technically accurate, it will have the appearance of a colossal lie to the student who has just attempted his first takeoff run and has experienced the typical first timer's ride which is described below.

The normal reaction is that the beginner gradually advances the throttle, sees the airplane straying to the left, applies some right rudder, notices that it has no effect (because there isn't enough air-stream past the rudder yet), and adds more right rudder until he has it against the stop. By this time (less time than it takes for you to read this) the rudder has increased in effectiveness and we now have way too much rudder applied. Hence the sickening drift to the left has been replaced by a much faster lurch to the right. He now realizes this error, backs off on the right rudder and concludes that he can now control this unexpected monster. Yet at the precise moment he feels that he has control, he makes his second mistake. He raises the tail. Instantly, the torque due to P-factor disappears and is replaced by a momentary impulse of torque due to gyroscopic effect of the prop. This impulse suddenly forces him to the left again and this time he swears that he won't let the airplane control him and cranks in much right rudder. However, he is too late with too much. The torque impulse was only momentary, only present while the tail was being raised and then instantly disappeared. His right rudder actually materialized only after the torque had subsided, hence the airplane heads for the bushes again, this time to the right.

By this time, if the pilot is lucky, the airplane will have reached flying speed, and will have left the ground unscathed (probably heading 30 degrees to the right or left of the runway center line) with arrogant impatience at the five thumbs holding the stick.

I don't recall how many takeoffs I made that way in the old Aeronca Champ, headed straight for Louie's bedroom window, but it had to be quite a few before I learned how to control that infernal torque.

TORQUE—REVISITED

The secret, of course, is to realize that the torque correction is not constant. It must be made to vary identically as the torque itself varies. And so for this reason, we look at the torque elements and paint a composite picture of what the total torque will be.

In Figure 5.1a, we have a graph showing how the torque due to the

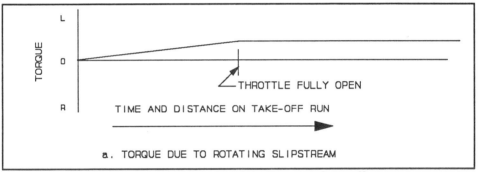

Figure 5.1a Taildragger torque due to rotating slipstream

rotating slipstream builds up. You can see that it reaches a fairly constant value by the time the throttle is fully opened.

In Figure 5.1b, the torque due to P-Factor builds up until the tail has been raised to the normal flight attitude. At this time, torque due to P-Factor drops to zero and remains at zero until the nose is raised to fly the airplane off. At this point, the airplane is in a climb attitude and torque again exists due to P-Factor.

Page 75

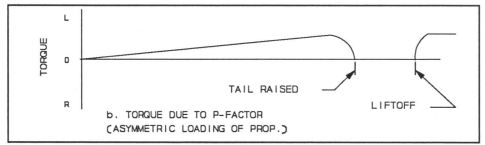

Figure 5.1b Taildragger torque due to P-Factor

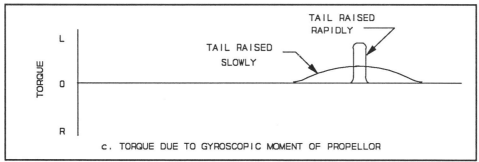

Figure 5.1c Taildragger torque due to gyroscopic moment

The torque due to the gyroscopic precession of the prop is shown in Figure 5.1c. Note that it is only present while the tail is <u>being raised</u>. Note also the solid line showing that it is of much greater amplitude and of shorter duration if the tail is raised quickly. The dotted line shows that the torque is much less but of longer duration if the tail is raised slowly.

Finally, Figure 5.1d shows the composite torque present when the three previously mentioned components are added together. Combine

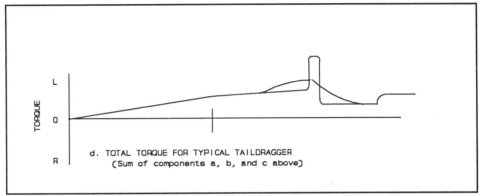

d. TOTAL TORQUE FOR TYPICAL TAILDRAGGER
(Sum of components a, b, and c above)

Figure 5.1d Composite torque for taildragger

this with the fact that the rudder sensitivity increases constantly as the airspeed increases, and that tail wheel steering is lost as soon as the tail is lifted off the ground, and it becomes quite clear why the compensation must be constantly varied. Hence, the fancy footwork required.[2]

The foregoing discussion has not been intended to discourage prospective taildragger pilots, nor is it intended that the pilot should attempt his first taildragger takeoff while reading a handful of instruction notes and charts. Rather, it is intended to provide him with enough knowledge to understand what is happening and why. In this way he may be able to master the takeoff maneuver in two or three tries rather than ten or twenty.

---

[2] Torques shown are for engines mounted in tractor configuration, and with clockwise rotation as seen from the cockpit. For reverse engine rotation, all curves must be reversed.

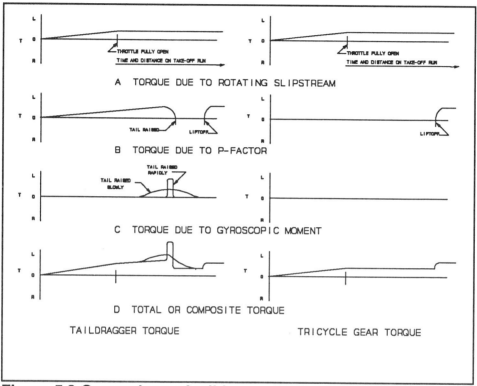

Figure 5.2 Comparison of taildragger and tricycle gear torque

If we compare the torque curves just discussed with the equivalent torque commonly experienced in a tricycle gear, we find that the torque component due to P-Factor (as in Figure 5.1b) and that due to gyroscopic precession of the propeller (as in Figure 5.1c) are essentially absent (see the right hand side of Figure 5.2). Hence, the resulting torque component is nothing more than that due to the rotating slipstream as in Figure 5.1a. If we compare the curve in

Figure 5.1a with that in Figure 5.1d, it is instantly obvious why the tricycle gear pilot has difficulty adjusting to the torque of the taildragger on takeoffs. When the instructor begins to explain the torque picture to him, the student of course notes his word, thinking all along that he knows all about torque because he already has 200 hours in Cherokees, etc., all the while having a mental image of the curve of Figure 5.1a. The taildragger instructor all this time has had the curve of Figure 5.1d in mind, and it isn't until the first takeoff that the student discovers the errors in his mental image of torque.

A brief examination of Figure 5.2 comparing the torque for both types of airplanes shows the simplicity of the torque correction required for the tricycle gear. Little wonder that the beginning pilot taking his initial instruction in tricycle gear learns torque control very quickly.

The astute reader will notice that we have not mentioned Reaction Torque as a torque component in the treatment just given. This omission is intentional, based on the fact that reaction torque is small compared with the other factors which were mentioned. It is of significant value only when an engine of high horsepower is accelerated very rapidly , as with an abrupt throttle movement. Since this is not a recommended procedure, we can neglect the discussion of Reaction Torque with relative safety.

The preceding discussion has not been meant to imply that an engineering degree is a prerequisite to flying taildraggers. Nothing could be further from the truth. For there are taildragger pilots who have flown very well for years without being able to explain the why's and wherefore's of their footwork during the takeoff run. They obviously learned to fly by practicing until they had developed the ability to do the right thing at the right time without necessarily understanding why. Most of these people would have learned much faster with a proper explanation of the factors involved. I know that I certainly would have. I also recall that very little ground school was available, which means that the bulk of the explanation of torque took place while walking out to the airplane. It can be summarized by the typical instructor's statement "you'll have to watch out for torque on the takeoff run and control it with plenty of right rudder". End of ground school!

If we summarize the control movements during the normal takeoff, we have the following:

1. Advance the throttle to full open while feeding the right amount of rudder to keep the airplane straight.

2. Forward stick to raise the tail while momentarily adding more right rudder to compensate for the gyroscopic precession of the propeller.

3. Slight back stick and small addition of right rudder while the airplane flies itself off the ground.

The differences between the taildragger takeoff and the tricycle gear, extend to more than torque. A secondary but none the less important difference is the feel of takeoff speed through the controls.

In a taildragger, because of the necessity to raise the tail during the takeoff run, the speed reached is instantly known to the pilot by the sensitivity of the elevators transmitted through the control system. Hence, the taildragger pilot does not normally check the airspeed indicator prior to lifting the airplane off the ground because he already knows the speed. He can feel it. This allows him to devote his full attention outside the cockpit where it is better spent in maintaining a straight course. The tricycle gear pilot, on the other hand, has no such speed cue through the controls since the elevators are not required to keep the tail up (the tricycle landing gear does that very nicely without assistance). The pilot therefore usually pays a bit more attention to the airspeed indicator at the moment of rotation. This is a disadvantage of tricycle gear, which really shows up when the short-field takeoff is compared between our two airplane configurations.

Perhaps the fear most often experienced by taildragger pilots is that of raising the tail too high during the takeoff run with consequent danger of the propeller striking the ground and possible nosing over. There is no need to be so alarmed since the tail height is very easy to control.

Since all other takeoff types are based on the normal takeoff, it is important that this maneuver be mastered before the other more specialized variations are attempted.

Finally, it should be noted that some taildragger airplane types, especially those with excellent takeoff performance, can be poor trainers. Typical of this category are the Cessna L-19 Birddog of Army fame and the Piper Super Cub. In both of these types, there is so much horsepower available, making it possible for the student to fly the airplane off before the tail has been raised and even before the throttle is fully opened. In such a case, the pilot will not learn the finer points of torque control because he's not likely to be on the ground long enough. Likewise, the combination of today's wide runways and high horsepower will often allow a takeoff without striking runway lights even after the airplane has veered away from the runway heading by as much as 30 or 40 degrees. In either case, a reduction in horsepower would increase the takeoff roll giving the student more time to find his feet. This is one of the reasons why airplanes like the 65 hp. Cubs and Champs were (and still are) such good trainers. They required the student to live with his mistakes for the duration of the takeoff run. On a hot day, this could be a considerable length of time.

It should be pointed out that a takeoff from a three point attitude, while often easier for the beginner because of the retention of tail wheel control right up to the moment of flight, is in reality danger-ous and is to be avoided as a regular procedure. The combination of high angle of attack and low speed borders on a stall condition and should be left to pilots with greater experience in the aircraft. Even then, it should be avoided in conditions other than relatively smooth air. In this kind of tail-low takeoff in gusty winds, the airplane has a tendency to leave the ground riding a gust, and will suddenly return to ground as soon as said gust quits. The return will not be as gentle as the departure.

SHORT FIELD TAKEOFF

The short field takeoff differs slightly from the normal takeoff. The two major differences to bear in mind are:

1. The tail is raised less than for a normal takeoff.

2. The airplane will be flown off at a lower airspeed and with poorer control responses.

In the case of Item 2 above, this is no different than for the equivalent takeoff in a tricycle geared airplane. On the other hand, Item 1 requires some judgment to raise the tail wheel only a few inches (4 to 6 inches) off the ground.

The short field takeoff procedure is then as follows:

1. Line up the airplane with the runway and let it roll forward just enough to center the tail wheel.

2. Hold the airplane with brakes, and with the stick back, gradually apply full power.

3. Release the brakes and as speed picks up let the elevator control streamline itself. Steer the airplane to hold it straight.

4. If necessary, apply slight forward stick to raise the tail off the ground 4 to 6 inches. In some airplanes, the tail may rise of its own accord without control input depending on weight, C.G. location, and elevator trim setting.

5. Allow the airplane to fly itself off in this attitude.

6. Proceed to achieve best angle of climb speed (V_x) as soon as possible for the climb segment until obstructions have been cleared.

The pilot must guard against attempting to raise the tail prematurely. The application of forward stick too early will contribute nothing more than drag thereby significantly increasing the takeoff run.

It should be pointed out that the "feel" which the pilot will receive through the elevator control will eventually become a more accurate and automatic (to the point of becoming subconscious) indication of airspeed than the airspeed indicator. This is a decided advantage of the breed, and is one of the reasons why the taildragger is preferred by the elite short-field specialist, the bush pilot.

The use of flaps has not been mentioned since it differs so much for the individual airplane models. As in the case of the tricycle gear, the Pilot's Operating Handbook recommendation should be followed.

SOFT FIELD TAKEOFF

In departing from a soft field, it is important that the tail not be raised in order to prevent the airplane from nosing over when patches of soft ground or mud are encountered. This is accomplished by holding the tail down with the elevators throughout most of the takeoff run. Of course, care must be taken to be sure that an excessive amount of back elevator isn't used. This could be detrimental in two ways. It could delay the takeoff by imposing unnecessary loads on the tail wheel and increasing drag, and it could also result in the airplane's leaving the ground in an excessively nose high attitude. The latter is extremely dangerous and could result in a stall close to the ground.

On a step by step basis then, we have the following:

1. Lower the flaps as recommended in the airplane's flight manual.

2. Gradually apply full power and insure that the takeoff roll is straight. (This may not be easy since one wheel may roll through soft ground or mud while the other is on firm ground).

3. Maintain the stick slightly aft of neutral to keep the tail down. Should both main wheels appear to bog down, it may be necessary to apply full back elevator. Also, in those rare instances when both wheels get bogged down enough that it is impossible to taxi forward, the wheels may sometimes be loosened by alternate rapid applications of full rudder on each side. However, this is a very delicate maneuver, to be accomplished with the finesse of mating porcupines.

4. As the airplane approaches flying speed, back elevator pressure should be relaxed in preparation for the takeoff.

5. When the airplane leaves the ground, it is leveled off until it accelerates to the best rate of climb speed (V_y).

6. Proceed with the climb.

Crosswind takeoffs are treated in a Chapter 7, "Crosswind Operations".

6

LANDINGS

The art of landing a taildragger in the absence of crosswinds is easily learned provided that a few basic principles are understood. We will begin by discussing these, and then we will proceed with the entire landing sequence.

Two basic landing types are used in taildraggers, each of which has its distinct advantages and disadvantages. Also, where it may appear on the surface that the landing types are interchangeable, this is not quite true most of the time although there are many times when the pilot can take his choice. This will be when conditions don't dictate a particular choice for him.

The two types of landings are the three point landing and the wheel landing. The three pointer is generally used in the following circumstances:

- Training - During early training, the pilot must learn the three pointer because it is easier to learn than the wheel landing. Hence, the wheel landing is postponed until a later training stage.

- Short Field - The shortest possible landing in most taildraggers can best be accomplished as a three pointer. It allows a slightly lower approach speed to be used (there are exceptions).

- Soft Field - Again, the landing at the lowest possible speed is made as a three pointer.

The wheel landing must be used when the winds are high and or gusty, especially if the wind is across the runway as well. It is used because it gives the pilot much more control at the instant of touch-down. The price of wheel landings is a slightly longer landing run due to the slightly higher approach speed required, hence, in most taildraggers the wheel landing is not used for short fields.

THREE POINT LANDING

The simplest approach to the three point landing is to consider that the airplane is flown parallel and close to the ground as long as possible until it stalls and settles to the ground of its own accord. At that time it will settle to the ground three point regardless of the type of airplane, type of landing gear (provided it is of taildragger configuration), etc. It should be remembered though that the stick should be all the way back at the time of contact (or nearly so) and should be held there through most of the landing roll. If the above is understood and followed, there will be no bounce because the conditions conducive to generating bounces will be absent.

This brings us to the most misunderstood phenomena in all of taildragger flying. The bounce. I am firmly convinced that many (if not most) of the taildragger pilots—including their instructors —believe the bounce to be caused by the spring and shock absorber in the landing gear. Nothing could be further from the truth. We would all be much better off if the bounce had originally been called a jounce. This would force pilots to try to understand it, and would be much less misleading.

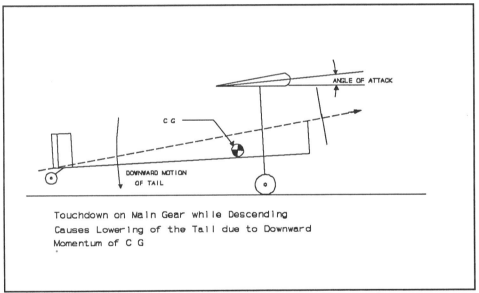

figure 6.1a Taildragger initiating a bounce (jounce)

The classic bounce occurs because the pilot attempted a three point landing and allowed the main gear to touch first. Hence, the airplane was not in a three point attitude at the time of contact. Let us examine it closely.

In Figure 6.1a, the pilot has been flying the airplane parallel with the runway surface waiting for it to stall. However, he did not apply a continued increase in back elevator as he should have as the airspeed diminished and the bounce was created as follows:

1. As the airplane slowed, lift was reduced. Remember that lift depends on speed and angle of attack. As speed is reduced, angle of attack must be increased in order to maintain lift.

2. When the lift was reduced, the airplane came down and contacted the ground on the main landing gear as shown in Figure 6.1a.

3. At the moment of contact, the tail has a tendency to continue downward due to the downward velocity of the C.G., and due to the fact that the C.G. is aft of the main landing gear.

4. This downward motion of the tail results in an increase in angle of attack as shown in Figure 6.1b. This in turn increases lift, and with the new amount of lift present, the airplane is able to fly again and that is precisely what it does. It can go to 10, 20, or even 50 feet depending on the severity of the bounce which determines the amount of increase in angle of attack.

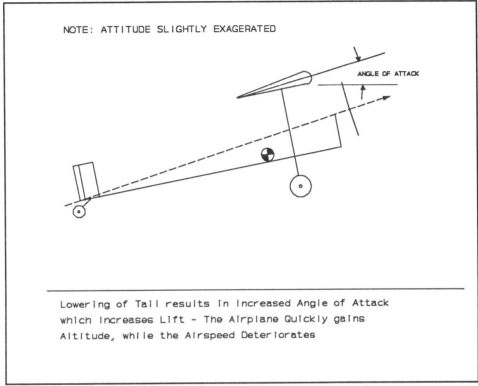

NOTE: ATTITUDE SLIGHTLY EXAGERATED

ANGLE OF ATTACK

Lowering of Tail results in Increased Angle of Attack
which Increases Lift - The Airplane Quickly gains
Altitude, while the Airspeed Deteriorates

Figure 6.1b Taildragger bounce (jounce) realized

The sage observers watching the above are likely to claim that the pilot struck the ground too hard, and that the spring in the landing gear caused the bounce. However, these same individuals would be surprised if they should see an airplane with hard gear (landing gear without springs or shock absorbers as in many of our smaller homebuilts) bounce just as high as a Cessna with its "terrible" spring gear.

Of course, when the airplane reaches the top of the bounce it is now very close to a stall. Remember that its angle of attack was increased but that the speed wasn't. In fact, it has been constantly loosing speed due to drag. Hence it stalls and sometimes with undesirable consequences.

For the sake of comparison, Figures 6.2a and b show a tricycle geared airplane which touches down with a slight vertical velocity. Here the downward momentum of the C.G. will lower the nose after touchdown thereby decreasing lift. The airplane is now on the ground to stay.

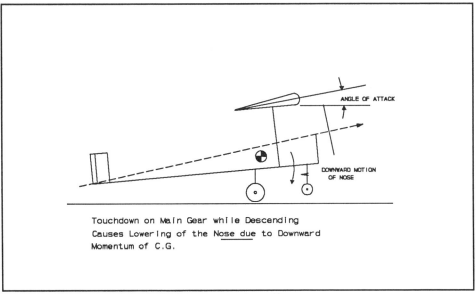

Figure 6.2a Typical tricycle gear landing.

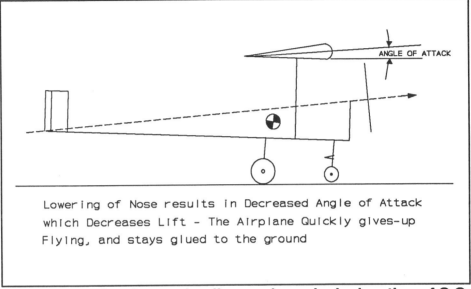

ANGLE OF ATTACK

Lowering of Nose results in Decreased Angle of Attack which Decreases Lift - The Airplane Quickly gives-up Flying, and stays glued to the ground

Figure 6.2b Tricycle gear landing made easier by location of C.G. forward of main gear.

Let's now look at the sequence for a typical taildragger three-point landing.

1. The approach is no different whether the airplane is tricycle geared or taildragger.

2. The airplane is gradually flared out close to the ground —within a foot or so.

3. A serious attempt is made to keep the airplane flying as long as possible by gradually easing back the elevator to maintain the proximity to the ground without touching. This must be a continuous motion.

4. When the airplane finally stalls, it will drop to the ground on all three wheels and must be guided straight throughout the roll-out.

5. The stick must be held full back and not released as is typical of tricycle gear landings.

6. Brakes should not be applied unless needed, and then only sparingly and with a pumping motion.

If the airplane is close to the ground when it stalls in Step 4 above, it may bounce. But bear in mind that if it strikes the ground three point, the bounce will be very mild and will seldom be more than a foot or two. The solution to this type of bounce is to hold the stick all the way back and ride it through the bounce. The common error here is that the pilot relaxes the back elevator pressure during the bounce. The tail then rises, tail wheel steering is lost, and the airplane heads for the bushes in one direction or other.

The common mistakes made by the tyro are those already mentioned namely, the bounce or jounce, and failure to hold the stick all the way back. The latter is so typical of the tricycle gear pilot transitioning to taildraggers and probably exists because of the habit of relaxing back elevator at the moment of touchdown in a tricycle geared airplane. This procedure is proper for the tricycle gear type because, with the C.G. forward of the main gear (see Figure 6.2), the effect is to reduce the angle of attack and glue the airplane to the ground as in Figure 6.2b. It also puts the nose wheel on the ground, thereby providing steering.

A word of caution to the transitioning pilot. It is customary among many tricycle gear pilots to relax immediately after touchdown and let the airplane—like the milkman's old nag—find its own way to the parking spot while he devotes his attention to cockpit tasks such as shutting down electronics, etc. and filling out the logs. To indulge in this practice in a taildragger is to invite disaster. The airplane must be guided all the way to a stop. The taildragger landing is somewhat easier than the takeoff because of the relative absence of torque. However, where torque was the bugaboo on takeoff, wind is the culprit on landing. This is so because of the absence of engine thrust which makes the airplane less controllable and therefore more susceptible to wind gusts. If the gust is aligned with the runway, it tends to mask the timing with which the airplane develops the stall. On the other hand, if the gust is across the runway, it can easily turn a good landing into an outright catastrophe. More on this in Chapter 7 which deals with crosswinds.

Let's discuss for a moment some of those factors which can make the three point landing in a taildragger a bit difficult.

In some aircraft, the force required on the stick to reach the three point attitude is quite high. The J-3 Cub is a good example. In this type of airplane, a young pilot or one of slight build may have to place both hands on the stick to get the tail all the way down. This is one example of an airplane in which a lady pilot, especially one of petite stature, may run out of muscle. Also, in some types the nose blocks off so much forward visibility when in a near three point attitude that the pilot becomes leery of raising the nose any higher. Such airplanes as the J-3 Cub (flown from the rear seat) and the Cessna 190 - 195 series are good examples of this. Next we have some airplanes in which springiness of the landing gear can contribute a rolling motion to the bounce or jounce making directional control more difficult. Typical is the Cessna L-19 Birddog of Korean War fame. This airplane is long legged, sitting high off the ground, and, if three pointed just a bit high, will bounce more than average, with a tendency to head right or left at around the third bounce. This tendency will be seriously aggravated by relaxation of back elevator pressure which will cause the tail to bob up and down. It is during one of these "bobs" that directional control will be lost. Bear in mind that what we've discussed here is not a contradiction of what we said earlier regarding the jounce. This bounce is not caused by springy landing gear. It was created by landing the airplane high and dropping it in. Then, once created, the bounce can certainly be aggravated by the springy landing gear. This type of bounce which is spring induced rarely exceeds a foot or two in height. While this can still create a problem, it is mild by comparison with the aerodynamically induced "jounce" which can easily exceed 10 or 20 feet.

RECOVERY FROM A BOUNCE

It is very important that the student learn the proper recovery procedure for the bounced landing attempt. From previous descriptions of the bounce (jounce), it should be obvious that the position of the airplane at the peak of the bounce is a precarious one. If the pilot takes no remedial action at this stage and attempts to ride through the bounce, the result will be a very hard landing which is likely to damage the airplane.

Depending on the altitude, air speed, and pilot's skill, a couple of choices exist. Namely:

1. Application of full throttle for an immediate go-around.

2. Let the airplane descend and flare again when close to the ground. This will be accomplished safely only if sufficient air speed exists, probably because the original approach and flare were attempted at excessive speed.

3. If insufficient air speed exists for item 2. above, the pilot may apply sufficient power to prevent a stall, allow the airplane to descend and flare again for a landing.

In either of these choices, the pilot must ensure that the throttle is advanced "smartly", which means quickly but <u>not abruptly</u>. This is no time for hesitation on the part of the pilot. Yet, abrupt throttle use <u>must be avoided</u> because

- This is no way to treat an engine.

- The Cessna L-19 Birddog and the P-51 Mustang (and probably many other types) have been known to snap-roll when treated in this manner.[1]

TAIL FIRST LANDING

The question is often raised by transitioning pilots as to the possible dangers of making a stall landing during which the tail wheel strikes the ground before the main wheels do. The answer is simply that there is nothing wrong with this maneuver because it is not likely to create a jounce or bounce. The reason for this is that when the tail wheel contacts the ground, either one of the two following actions will take place:

1. The tail wheel will immediately bounce off the ground resulting in a decrease in the angle of attack with resulting loss of lift.

2. The tail wheel will stay on the ground and downward momentum of the C.G. will cause the main wheels to descend closer to the ground.

In either case, the result is that the angle of attack is decreased immediately following the first contact with the ground. This will precipitate a reduction in lift, hence the airplane will soon rest solidly on the ground. Note that this is the exact opposite of what

---

[1] The Surgeon General says that snap-rolls in the flare may be dangerous to your health.

happens in a jounce. (In that case, the angle of attack and lift were both increased, causing the airplane to lift off the ground).

It should be pointed out here that while acceptable, the tail-first landing is a seldom seen maneuver simply because of the large amount of back elevator control required. In fact, I'm sure that we could find a number of taildraggers which cannot be landed tail-first because full back elevator at landing speeds will barely bring the nose up to a three point attitude. This of course would depend on load conditions and C.G. location.

As a final note, the tail-first landing is not a recommended procedure for two good reasons. The first is that it can generate a bit of a crow-hop down the runway with the tail wheel being alternately in the air and then on the ground. Were this to happen to a beginner, he could lose directional control during the moments when the tail wheel is airborne. The likelihood of this occurring will increase if the back elevator control is relaxed. The way to ride through such a crow-hop without incident is to maintain the stick full back (as it should be for any three-point landing).

The second reason for suggesting that tail-first landings shouldn't be performed deliberately is that it tends to be abusive of the equipment. Tail wheels tend to be sensitive to shock, and this type of landing can provide significant shock to the tail structure, especially if the above mentioned crow-hop is excited. As an example, one airplane type which has suffered from this type of activity is the previously mentioned Cessna Birddog. Most of the Birddogs which survived the training duties with the U.S. Army have had tail wheel assemblies replaced one or more times, and in many cases tail springs were also replaced due to breakage.

WHEEL LANDING

We have now reached the maneuver which is without a doubt the most difficult to learn by a transitioning pilot. That is the wheel landing. In fact, the patience required of both student and instructor regarding this maneuver is so high that many check-outs are terminated (aborted would be a better word) after a dozen or so attempts at wheel landings with the instructor's final comment being "go ahead and get the feel of the airplane shooting three point landings and we'll get to the wheel landings later". The instructor then quickly departs while contemplating a legal change of name, change of address, unlisted phone number, or in extreme cases, will consider flying pipeline patrol in Oklahoma.

If your taildragger checkout ended this way, it is unfortunate since you were short changed and have been left high and dry with an incomplete checkout. The price you will pay (or have paid) for this is a serious limitation in your use of the taildragger. There will be days when wind conditions will render the wheel landing mandatory simply because the stall landing will result in a bent airplane. These wind conditions are high and gusty winds as well as gusty cross-winds. Now it's well for you to say that you won't fly on days such as this. However, this begs the question of how will you manage to land if the wind got stirred up while you were airborne? You can't always carry enough fuel to last through until tomorrow.

In summary, anything less than a complete taildragger checkout is a farce placing you in the position of an accident waiting for a place to happen. And a complete checkout includes proficiency in wheel landings.

Now, back to the wheel landing. Note that I mentioned that the wheel landing is difficult to learn. It is also difficult to teach. (When you are sweating out the learning it may be comforting to know that the instructor is sweating out the teaching.) However, I did not say that the wheel landing is a difficult maneuver to perform simply because it isn't. In fact, if you had been around a generation ago to watch the local pros shooting wheelies in the old twin Beech 18's or DC-3's, it would have appeared to be the easiest maneuver in the world. The pros use this type of landing so much because, once learned, it is so easy to perform.

Let's begin by listing the advantages of wheel landings. They include the following:

1. Maximum controllability of the airplane through the touchdown point.

2. Reduced susceptibility to being blown about by wind gusts.

3. Improved visibility during the landing run.

4. Ability to set the airplane on the ground at any speed desired (within reason) above stall speed.

5. Ease of transition from one taildragger type or model to another.

6. Safety in the face of unknowns such as:

    a) Night landings in poor visibility

    b) Overloaded airplane

    c) Airplane iced up such that exact stall speed is unknown.

And finally, let's remember the most important advantage, which is that on some days there is no other way to get the airplane on the ground in one piece. Hence the wheel landing is not a luxury. It is a basic necessity and should be approached as such.

Next, if we look at the reasons why the wheel landing is difficult to learn, we find the following two to be outstanding:

1. The wheel landing procedure is the exact opposite of the three pointer procedure. Hence it requires that much of the previous learning be reversed, and this is always difficult.

2. Most instructors begin the wheel landing instruction in the airplane. This is the wrong place. It should be started at the blackboard.

3. An exaggerated fear that forward elevator will cause the propeller to strike the runway.

To begin with, the wheel landing is executed by letting the airplane contact the ground on the main wheels followed by an <u>immediate</u> application of forward elevator to reduce the angle of attack and keep the wheels glued on. Sounds simple? It is.

Secondly, a useful training exercise to convince the student that the fear in item 3 above is of little concern, is to raise the tail of a light taildragger, say a J-3 or Aeronca champ to a level flight attitude with the tail placed on a saw-horse. With the student inside the airplane, the view in a wheel landing attitude can then be experienced and memorized. The student can then climb out of the airplane and see, to his surprise, how much propeller ground clearance remains. Naturally, it may not be possible to perform this in the heavier taildraggers.

If we digress for a moment and review the three point landing, remember that the jounce was created by downward motion of the tail after the main wheels touched ground. In reading that section, a reasonably clever student would be inclined to ask "why not push the stick forward when the main wheels touch down thereby raising the tail, reducing the angle of attack, and decreasing lift. Won't this keep the airplane on the ground"? The answer to that question would be "Eureka! You've just re-invented the wheel landing". Of course we should also mention that during the roll-out, the stick should be gradually pushed forward to keep the tail up as the airplane slows down. More and more forward elevator is required for this, and once the stick reaches full forward, the tail will finally drop of its own accord. Remember that if the tail is allowed to drop prematurely, the angle of attack will increase, the lift will increase, and the airplane could leave the ground. On the other hand, when the tail drops at the end of roll-out, the speed is so low that the increased angle of attack is inconsequential.

Let's run through the entire procedure again on a step by step basis.

1. Perform a normal approach at normal approach speeds.

2. In the early part of flare-out, let the main wheels contact the ground with minimum downward velocity (rate of descent). It may be advisable to carry some power until the touchdown point, at least during training since this seems to help beginners. However, beware of carrying too much.

3. Immediately apply forward stick to keep the airplane on the ground. The required amount of forward stick will be small if the downward momentum (rate of descent) of the airplane was small. Remove (ease it off) the power which was carried through the approach.

4. Continue increased applications of forward stick to keep the tail up until it descends of its own accord with full stick forward.

5. Once the tail has lowered to the ground, apply full back elevator to keep the tail wheel on the ground.

Finally, some comments pertaining to the above listed steps are in order. In the case of Step 1, a myth which has long been perpetuated and which has been the source of a great deal of confusion pertaining to wheel landings is that the approach must be made at much higher speed than for a three pointer. This is not true. While there certainly will be days when the wheel landing will be made at speeds above the normal landing speeds, this will be due to the presence of strong or gusty winds. Hence the speed is necessitated by the weather and not by the type of landing. If the normal approach speed in your taildragger is 65 mph, there is no need to increase it for wheel landings. This statement is true for most light taildraggers, but exceptions can be found. In fact, there is no need to decide on the type of landing to be made until the tires are inches from the ground. A good "think-fast" exercise for the advanced student is for the instructor to wait until the airplane has passed the runway threshold before informing the student of the type of landing to be made.

If the wheel landing is attempted at unnecessarily high speeds, the end result is that the pilot is discouraged from trying wheel landings again because of the excessive runway length thus required. Also, in such a case the pilot has a tendency to "hurry" the airplane and—as he sees the runway flashing by—forces the airplane to the ground before it is ready to land. The result is generally unprintable.

With respect to Step 3, the questions most often asked are "how high must the tail be raised" and "won't the prop hit the ground"? The answer to the first is that the amount is not really important. For a typical light taildragger, it is not important whether the tail is raised half an inch or five inches. The important point is that it be raised a positive amount in a firm motion. Remember that the object of lifting the tail is the reduction of angle of attack and lift in order to keep the airplane on the ground (prevent a jounce). And in order to accomplish this, it is only necessary to lose some lift. The amount lost does not have to be great. Hence the tail doesn't have to be raised very far. In a perfectly executed wheel landing, the amount through which the tail was actually raised may not be noticeable to the passengers, even if they are experienced pilots. The answer to the second question is that this fear is grossly exaggerated. In real life, there is sufficient ground clearance to prevent the prop from chewing the concrete. (Except of course in such warbirds as the Curtis P-40 or the P-51 Mustang and the like where some extra caution may be desired.)

The errors most often made when the wheel landing is attempted are as follows:

1. Failure to apply forward stick at the time the main wheels contact the ground.

2. Attempt to land with excessive downward velocity (rate of descent). Failing to level the airplane and check the rate of descent which was carried earlier in the approach.

3. Use of excessively high speeds and/or excessive power.

4. Diving at the runway. This is nearly the same as item 2, except that in this case it is a "desperation" play.

The first of these is by far the most common and stems from the fact that during all the previous landings the pilot was lectured about the necessity for pulling the stick all the way back. Suddenly, he is told to push it forward. This requires a recycling of the learning curve. The second reason, as mentioned previously is the fear that the prop will strike the ground. In fact, if the prop ever does hit the ground during a wheelie, the chances will be that error number 2 above was the reason. Cessna's with their spring gear are more prone to this than are other taildraggers. In an ordinary airplane, a wheel landing with excessive downward velocity will be a hard landing, but often without ill effect if the pilot recovers in time or executes a go-around. In a Cessna, the landing gear will spread—and spread—until the prop hits the ground. Quite often, especially if this happened on a grass field, the pilot may not be aware of prop damage and continue shooting landings only to note—after he has parked the bird—that the prop tips are curled. The more creative pilots are known to invent new cuss words for the occasion. There is even a case on record of a Cessna 195 whose gear spread enough on impact for the belly to strike the ground. I mention this not to malign the Cessnas, but rather to show what can happen.

It should be borne in mind, that the reason forward stick is to be applied at the moment of impact is to counteract the downward momentum of the C.G. From this then, we can see that the higher the downward velocity, the greater the downward momentum of the C.G.. Hence, the greater the amount of forward stick required to counteract it. The result is that the student will have an easier time coping with the wheel landing if the ground is just kissed with minimum downward velocity. This also happens to be much easier on the tires and the airplane structure.

On the other hand, the pilot diving for the runway will probably hit the ground with the main gear while carrying a higher rate of descent than can be easily counteracted with forward elevator. The most likely result will be the initiation of a large jounce when the C.G.continues its downward motion and increases the angle of attack by a large amount. By this time, the airplane quickly leaves the ground with elan, and it becomes immaterial whether the botched landing had been intended as a three pointer or a wheel landing. In either case, the result and the cure are the same. The obvious result is a hopping flight path that is always difficult to bring under control.

The solution to all of this resides in a couple of choices. For the beginner, the best choice is usually a go-around with a return to try again. Whereas the experienced pilot may succeed in converting the botched wheel landing into a three pointer by a timely and smooth application of enough power to reestablish a decent flare if sufficient runway length remains.

This leads us to an often asked question which is "must power be used to make a wheel landing?" The answer is that power—in most taildraggers—is not necessary to make a good wheel landing, but that in many cases it does help. For example, most students have an easier time learning the wheel landing if they carry some power because it allows them to control the flare and the downward velocity more accurately. Hence, it is easier to teach wheel landings if power is used.

Likewise, it is easier to teach wheel landings if a long runway is used. This does not mean that a long runway is necessary for wheel landings. What it does mean is that the competent instructor will use power and long runways as teaching tools, and will later show the student that both are in fact unnecessary. The problem with teaching wheel landings on a short runway is that the student bringing the airplane into a short field with power suddenly realizes that the runway is going by at a good rate, and subsequently hurries through the wheel landing attempt. And we all know what excessive haste does to any learning situation. Conversely, a long runway gives him time to get things setup a bit more methodically.

Once the wheel landing is mastered, it is very important that it be practiced often, otherwise the skill will soon disappear from lack of use. To let the skill die is perhaps the biggest mistake many taildragger pilots make. I see this every year. Too many of the taildragger pilots I fly with respond to a request for a wheel landing with "but, I haven't made one in years". In fact, just a few weeks before writing this section, I asked a taildragger CFI to perform a wheel landing as part of his checkout in a particular airplane. He eyed the snow covered runway and replied "but I've never done them on anything but dry grass". They've allowed their skills to shrivel.

While it's easy to say that power is not a prerequisite of the wheel landing, this is of course a general statement. There may be some airplanes with certain C.G. location and/or flap configuration which preclude wheel landings without power. Obviously, one adjusts to these situations as they are encountered.

Finally, the epitome of taildragger skill is the ability to perform a wheel landing as easily as a three pointer without prior warning or preparation. In fact, the sharp taildragger pilot one day learns that it is possible to salvage a poor three point landing by quickly pushing the stick forward and converting it to a wheel landing. This really works[2].

SHORT FIELD LANDINGS

The short field landing in a taildragger is similar to that in a trike. The approach is generally the same, hence needs no explanation. The actual landing however, is usually three point since this ensures the lowest possible speed at the time of ground contact. As soon as the airplane is rolling on the ground, the elevators are held in the full up position and the brakes can be pumped, usually in an alternating sequence. Should the airplane show signs of wanting to nose-over from too much braking, a blast of throttle will often rectify the situation and force the tail down. As in the tricycle gear, the flaps are raised as soon as possible after touchdown to increase the weight on the main wheels. If this is in a retractable geared airplane, double-check to be sure that the handle you actuate is the flap handle, and not the gear handle.

---

[2] I once wrote this in to one of our leading magazines, and their taildragger "expert" promptly wrote me that this was impossible because no one would be able to respond with the correct timing. Hogwash! Yet, years later I found that the exact procedure is recommended in Reference 15.

SOFT FIELD LANDINGS

The soft field landing is performed like the short field version except that the application of brakes is omitted. Some power is generally carried because it allows the airplane to be flown at its slowest speed. Also, flaps retraction should be left until the airplane has stopped. Here again, should the tail come up inadvertently say, due to soft ground, a judicious application of throttle with full back stick may force the tail back down.

7

CROSSWIND OPERATIONS

The previous chapters have covered normal takeoff's and landings as well as the differences between the taildragger and the tricycle geared airplane. We have seen the differences in stability as a function of landing gear configuration. In this chapter, we will cover the most demanding of the maneuvers, namely those arising from crosswind operations. The crosswind and its effect on the stability of the airplane when it is at the air to ground interface is probably responsible for more taildragger landing accidents than any other single factor.

The main reason for this is that, in the presence of a crosswind, the taildragger now becomes an entirely different animal, and what is more important, is that it becomes a tiger with even a slight crosswind. This is completely at variance with the trike.

In the case of the tricycle geared airplane, pilots habitually ignore crosswinds of, say five to eight knots with absolute impunity. This is not to say that they should, for most learned better at some stage of their training. The fact is however that in practice, ignoring a slight crosswind, though it does no good to the landing gear, generally does not result in an accident. In the taildragger, any amount of crosswind, if ignored and not compensated for, can quickly turn a passable landing into a catastrophe.

The principles spelled out in the preceding chapters don't change just because of the presence of a crosswind. Torque must still be corrected for on the takeoff, and drift must still be eliminated for the landing. In this chapter, we need to discuss the "how" portion in view of the fact that the presence of crosswinds adds a source of drift which contributes to directional difficulties in the flare and touch-down.

To begin with, if the crosswind is to be dealt with correctly, it must be known in terms of direction and velocity.

MEASURING THE CROSSWIND

Various means are available for assessing the direction and amplitude of crosswinds. At most airports, we have wind socks which should always be checked prior to any flight or ground operations. There are, of course, times when no wind sock is present, or, times when the wind sock will give inappropriate information. For example, at a large airport, a wind sock a mile away from the point of take off and landing shows the crosswind existing a mile away from the area of interest. This may coincide with the actual wind at the takeoff and landing point, but then again it may not.

One can also use smoke from nearby chimneys as a wind indicator, but here again it may not be near enough to be of sufficient accuracy.

Finally another excellent wind indicator is the crab angle which is required to maintain the required track on downwind, base and final. It is pointless to argue the merits and accuracies of the different sources of wind information. In fact, the final result is that the sharp taildragger pilot will use all the indicators available and constantly compare them with each other.

One note of caution is that unfortunately, all wind socks are not created equal. Hence, a light weight sock may be straight out at 10 knots, while a heavier one may not be straight out until 15 knots are reached.

It is also important to bear in mind that a difference in wind indications obtained from the above listed methods does not mean that they are inaccurate. Rather, it probably means that the wind is indeed different at the particular locations of the wind indicators, and that in itself is a warning to be on the lookout for shifty winds, turbulence, and wind shear. Let's go on to the crosswind takeoff.

FLAP LIMITS IN CROSSWIND OPERATIONS

The overwhelming majority of the Pilot's Operating Handbooks for general aviation airplanes mention that "a limited amount of flaps" should be used for crosswind operations. Most don't set a specific limit, leaving the decision to be based on the pilot's judgment and experience. This elusive minimum will of course depend on how much flap is available in the first place. For example, some airplanes have a reputation for flaps which are so small as to be nearly useless (at least when compared to larger flaps on other models). The Cessna

140 and 170 (1948 version) fall in that category. With such small flaps, the pilot is unlikely to have a problem in crosswinds even with full deflection. The later model Cessna's, on the other hand, are well known for their "barn doors". In these models, flap use in excess of 15 degrees will add considerable difficulty to the control of the airplane in crosswinds. Under such conditions, the less flap surface exposed the better. A good rule to follow is to limit the flaps to 10 degrees, or 1 notch, unless the POH or experience in the airplane dictate otherwise.

CROSSWIND TAKEOFF

The compensations for crosswind during takeoff are as simple as they are necessary. They can be summarized into the following steps:

1. Keep the windward wing down with aileron to keep the wind from getting under it and lifting it. This will require use of opposite rudder to keep the airplane tracking straight.

2. Keep the airplane straight on the takeoff run with the rudder. Additional rudder will be needed to overcome the weather-cocking caused by the crosswind.

3. Make the departure from the ground a positive one by initially raising the tail slightly more than for a normal takeoff so that the airplane can accelerate to a higher speed than normal before lift-off.

4. Once the departure from the ground is attained, relax rudder pressure to let the airplane turn into the wind to a proper crab angle and then level the wings.

Step 1 above is by far the most important of the series, and is the one usually forgotten.

To begin with, let's recognize that with the airplane in a level position, the windward wing will normally have more lift than the leeward wing unless something is done about it. This is due to the fact that the leeward wing is partially blanked out by the fuselage. This may not seem significant, but any difference in the lift created by each wing will result in an undesirable bank away from the wind unless corrective action is taken. This corrective action will be more effective when taken in anticipation, rather than after the fact.

The cure then is to apply the aileron control into the wind thereby raising the aileron on the windward wing. This move also has a dual effect. First, it will reduce the lift of the windward wing as much as possible even while both wings are still level, and secondly, when airspeed builds up, the air flow hitting the deflected ailerons will lower the wing. The correct procedure is to apply full aileron into the wind before the throttle is opened for the takeoff run, and to relax this aileron deflection as the airplane gains speed. The intended result is to keep the windward wing lowered without bringing it dangerously close to the ground.

Let's not forget that banking an airplane generally results in the initiation of a turn due to the tilted lift vector. And a turn at this point is exactly what we don't want. Rather, we wish to keep the airplane headed straight down the runway. Hence, we must apply opposite rudder resulting in a straight path but with controls crossed.

Step 3 is necessary to insure that the airplane leaves the ground only once; that is, without a momentary post-departure contact which, in the presence of a crosswind, will include a drift component. This is accomplished by raising the tail higher than normal during the takeoff run thereby allowing the airspeed to build up to a higher than normal value (due to the lower angle of attack) prior to lift-off. The higher than normal airspeed will ensure that the airplane stays in the air when it leaves the ground. In other words, it will ensure a "positive" lift-off.

We must remember throughout all this that control pressures will vary as airspeed builds up. As the takeoff roll begins, the aileron control will be held hard over. However, to leave it there throughout the takeoff run would be a disaster since the windward wing tip would soon drag the ground. The key of course is to command the windward wing to a certain wing low attitude and then to maintain that attitude with whatever aileron pressure is required.

Likewise, the airplane is to be kept on a straight path by whatever rudder pressure is required.

An important item should be mentioned at this point; one too often forgotten in our discussions. That is, that a crosswind takeoff, properly executed will require a longer takeoff run than normal. This is due to three very good reasons:

1. Reduced head wind component.

2. Reduced effective lift due to tilted lift vector (wing down).

3. Higher airspeed used due to the reduced angle of attack.

4. Additional drag due to crossed controls.

Since each one of the above can be significant, the total is usually appreciable. The net result is that ultra-short field operations should be avoided in a crosswind. Remember that the ground roll values quoted in the airplane owner's/operator's manual have not been compensated to reflect the above. Hence, in a crosswind, you're on your own.

COMMON ERRORS

One of the best ways of learning is to profit by the mistakes of others, so let me share with you the numerous errors I have seen during my travels as a check pilot.

The majority of crosswind takeoffs which go sour (and some which are barely salvaged at the last moment) begin with the pilot's complete ignorance of wind conditions, or at least a disregard for this important item. I've mentioned this earlier and feel that this common failing of so many of our pilots cannot be overemphasized.

The takeoff run starts without the pilot attempting to lower the windward wing either because he has forgotten this crucial step or because he has postponed it "until we get a bit of airspeed". In either case, this is an error.

If we assume that the crosswind is from the right for our example, we find that, without compensation, the right wing will be lifted slightly and the airplane will have a tendency to turn left due to the slight bank angle. At this point, nothing appears out of the ordinary to our pilot who may pat himself on the back for having discovered that the left turning tendency due to the left bank is nicely compensating for the airplane's desire to turn to the right—into the wind due to its weathervaning tendency.

Soon, the right wing will have enough lift to fly while the left wing will not. The right wheel comes off the ground with the airplane turning left and heading for the runway lights. In desperation, our hero "pulls" it off the ground—on the very edge of a stall. In this partial stall, he may clear the runway lights "in a single bound" if he is lucky. On the other hand, his sideways departure may appear like a stone skipping across a lake, with his landing gear skipping across the runway. If this is not his lucky day, one of these skips will be violent enough to generate a vicious ground loop to the right.

If he gets off the ground without damage, he will chuckle to himself that crosswind takeoffs are a bit dicey and will never realize the tremendous stresses which he has applied to the tires and other components of the landing gear. If he was not so fortunate and did indeed ground loop, you can bet that his explanation will begin with "everything was O.K. until.....". In either case, the pilot does not realize that his technique is incorrect.

In a slightly different version of the above, the right wing will lift and raise the right wheel off the ground. The wind from the right will strike the rudder and vertical fin and cause the airplane to weathervane and turn right. The combinations of these two actions along with the addition of centrifugal force will cause the left wing tip to drag the ground during the ensuing ground loop.

The reader who thinks that the above has been exaggerated need only talk to one or two A & P mechanics working on fabric covered taildraggers to develop some quick statistics regarding the incidence of broken wing tips found whenever one of these rag bags is unzipped for recovery. He will also learn why so many taildragger pilots prefer grass runways.

CROSSWIND LANDING

By comparison with the crosswind takeoff, the crosswind landing has all the appearances of a real bear. And yet, what makes it seem so difficult really rests in the imagination. For the landing like the takeoff is simple to perform once the proper procedures are known and followed.

The crosswind landing can be summarized in the following statement: "Keep the windward wing down as long as possible to prevent sidewards motion and perform the landing as any other." If a stall landing (three-pointer) was intended, it is still performed as a stall landing, although it has become a stall landing with a wing down. The touch-down is now a two-pointer (one main wheel and the tail wheel) rather than a three-pointer. The second main wheel will eventually touch down when the wing runs out of lift and aileron control thereby allowing the formerly raised wing to come down. Is this different from a similar landing (properly executed) in a tricycle geared airplane? No, it isn't much different. In either case, the airplane is brought to a stall with the windward wing down. In either case, the airplane goes through the flare and pre-landing gymnastics without knowing or caring whether it is a tail or nosedragger. In either case, the objective is the same, namely the elimination of drift prior to touching the ground.

On the other hand, if a wheel landing were desired, the comments concerning wheel landings in the previous chapter still apply. The difference is that the wheel landing is performed with the windward wing lowered, with the first contact made on a single main wheel. The second (upwind) main wheel will touch down when the airspeed has dropped sufficiently that the pilot is no longer able to maintain the windward wing lowered. Of course, by this time the aileron control will be against the stops. The tail wheel will also touch down shortly thereafter. This is not as difficult a procedure as it appears.

This may appear to be a gross oversimplification, but in fact is not. The pilot who has learned the correct principles of the normal taildragger landing will have no trouble adding crosswind compensation and following the same procedures. It is just that simple. And likewise, it can just as emphatically be said that the pilot who has not mastered the principles of the taildragger normal landing will not execute a crosswind landing without the accompaniment of the sounds of bending metal, etc.

Note that the above description of a crosswind landing is that of the "wing-down" type of landing. This is not the only type of crosswind landing which can be made. However, it is the best and safest method to use and the one recommended for use in general aviation taildraggers. For the sake of completeness, we will review all of the methods which are used, and point out their respective advantages, disadvantages, etc. in the hopes that the reader will be better able to critique what is printed in the popular magazines concerning crosswind landings.

While a great deal of material has been written and continues to be written in the monthly mags about the art of crosswind landings, not all of it can be properly applied to the landing of taildraggers. Let's briefly review and evaluate the procedures put forth.

In general,the over-abundant literature on the subject of crosswind landings lists three different "acceptable methods".

The first method is called the Wing-Down method. This consists of keeping the airplane's longitudinal axis aligned with the flight path and the runway by lowering the windward wing. If this sounds like the definition of a slip, it is precisely that, and therein lies its biggest disadvantage—the discomfort of passengers who may not know what is going on, and quickly conjure up visions of a crash because they just "know" that an airplane cannot be flown that way.

The second method is the Crab method. Using this technique, the pilot keeps the airplane following a straight path on final by turning it slightly into the wind and allowing it to "crab" as necessary. At the instant prior to touchdown the rudder is kicked to remove the crab. This ticklish maneuver is called de-crabbing. This type of approach is much more comfortable for the passengers who, being ignorant of crosswind procedures, don't appreciate the dangers inherent in the method nor the precise sense of timing required of the pilot.

The third method is usually called the Combination method. This consists of crabbing down the final and, when relatively close to the ground, transitioning to the "Wing-Down" method. This method has the decided advantage of minimizing the discomfort which the passengers would experience if the wing were to be kept down during the prolonged final approach.

In discussing the pro's and con's of the various methods, we will concern ourselves with the comparison of crab versus the wing down method, since we are interested in the dynamics of the airplane at the moment of touchdown. The combination method, because it ends as a "wing-down" landing, doesn't need much separate discussion.

WING-DOWN METHOD

Using this method, the pilot must establish a slip while he is on the final approach to the runway. He may not recognize it as such, but that is essentially what he is doing. By lowering the windward wing and applying the necessary amount of opposite rudder to keep the airplane going straight down the extended center line, he establishes a side slip such that the amount slipped to the side equals the amount the airplane drifts due to the crosswind. If the two are equal, the approach path will be straight, and, the airplane's longitudinal axis will be aligned with the runway at all times. In essence, all drift will have been canceled.

From the point of view of control mechanics, the wing down method is easily performed. First, the windward wing is lowered with the ailerons, and secondly, opposite rudder is applied to prevent the airplane from turning. The extent of wing down is easily measured. If the windward wing is not lowered sufficiently, the airplane will drift with the wind, and the path will not be in line with the runway. On the other hand, with the windward wing lowered excessively, the airplane will have a side slip component into the wind, and the path will not be in line with the runway. The amount of rudder to be used is determined simply by using whatever amount is necessary to prevent the airplane from turning in the direction of the lowered wing.

Once the proper amounts of aileron and rudder control are established, it is necessary to change them slightly but continuously as the airplane approaches the runway. The reason for this is twofold. First, as the airplane loses altitude, the amount of crosswind often varies. Hence the amount of slip must be regulated to remain equal to the amount of drift due to the crosswind. Secondly, as progress is made along the approach path, the airspeed usually decreases, and the drift angle for a given value of crosswind will increase thereby necessitating an increase in the component of slip. While all this may sound complicated, it is really quite simple. The visual cues available easily prevent over-controlling, and the pilot should not let himself be confused with the mechanics of the controls. This is a maneuver best done entirely by the "seat of the pants" technique.

As we now come to the flare and prepare for the landing, we are confronted with a choice as follows:

Do we touch down in a full stall, or do we perform a wheel landing? The answer is that we can do either, depending on the conditions. (Indeed, many tyro taildragger pilots have been known to do both).

If a stall landing is to be made, the lowered wing will be kept down throughout the flare and round-out, and what would normally be a three point landing will become a "two pointer" i.e., one main wheel and tail wheel. As the airplane settles on its two points, the pilot will gradually deflect the aileron control to the limits of its allowable travel in order to keep the lowered wing down as long as possible. In fact, a properly executed stall landing in a crosswind will normally be terminated with the aileron control hard-over into the wind. If such is not the case, then the pilot can conclude that he isn't doing it correctly. Note that the flare and stall, except for the lowered wing, are performed in the normal manner, and that the windward aileron correction must be maintained throughout the landing roll.

On the other hand, if we wish to terminate the approach in a wheel landing, the wheel landing is performed with the windward wing down as for a stall landing, hence the touchdown will be on one wheel only. Forward stick will be applied at the moment of touchdown to keep the tail up, and the aileron control will be progressively moved to keep the windward wing down, while simultaneously moving the stick forward to keep the tail up until the control reaches the limits. With stick control, the stick will end up in the right or left front corner. At this point, the tail will usually drop to the ground, and the stick is then brought straight back to keep the tail down, and the aileron deflection into the wind is maintained.

There will be situations where the choice of landing—wheel vs. stall—will be dictated by the current wind. Since the amount of wing down correction depends on the ratio of crosswind component to landing speed, the stall landing may require more wing down than control exists to provide it. Whereas, if a wheel landing is made, the higher speed may call for compensation which is within the control envelope, and differential braking may be used to augment the aerodynamic controls as the airplane slows down. This then, is an important advantage of the wheel landing.

Common Errors

The most common error in this type of landing is that the pilot is afraid to lower the wing sufficiently or to keep it lowered through the touchdown phase. There is a great tendency to let the wings become level at touchdown. The result is that the airplane will start drifting sideways as soon as the wings are level thereby spoiling what would have been a perfect landing.

Another oft committed error is the pilot's excessive concentration on keeping the windward wing lowered, and neglecting to keep the tail down. At the first bounce of the tail, the crosswind will pirouette the airplane into the wind and it will promptly head for the bushes. We must emphasize that the landing is completed with elevator control all the way back and with the aileron control hard over. In a stick controlled airplane, the stick ends up in the right or left rear corner.

Despite the warnings and admonitions on limiting flap use in crosswind conditions, this remains a common pilot error. The use of excessive flaps, especially in gusting crosswind conditions, creates control difficulties which can turn what could have been an acceptable landing into a poor one. Yet, the problem can so easily be avoided by limiting flap extension to 10 or 15 degrees. Pilots, read and heed your handbooks!

WING-DOWN CONCERNS

When crosswind landing methods are openly compared, we find that at least two concerns are expressed by pilots, and these are often used in arguments advocating the use of the crab method. The first concern is that of the use of a slip in conjunction with flap use in the various Cessna models placarded against slipping with flaps. The second deals with the apparent exposure to danger in the form of crossed controls at low airspeeds. Both of these concerns deserve discussion to place them in proper perspective.

Cessna Slip/Flap Problem

In the case of the Cessna flaps, the concerned pilots would tell us that by making a crosswind landing using the wing-down technique, we are violating the placard restrictions in the Cessna Pilot's Operating Handbook. But are we? An examination of the handbooks yields 2 examples of wording:

> " *Steep slips should be avoided with flap settings greater than 20   degrees......*" (Reference 16).

and,

> " *Avoid slips with flaps extended*" (Reference 17).

And then, in the section covering CROSSWIND LANDING, both of the above mentioned references state the following:

> " *When landing in a strong crosswind, use the minimum flap setting required for the field length. If flap settings greater than 20 degrees are used in sideslips with full rudder deflection, some elevator oscillation may be felt at normal approach speeds..........Although the crab or combination method of drift correction may be used, the wing-low method gives the best control.*" (References 16 and 17)

In essence, the combination of the above tells us that the problem with slips and flaps occurs when slips are steep, and with large flap deflections. Yet, Cessna recommends that the minimum flap setting be used (normally interpreted as 10 to 15 degrees by most Cessna pilots) and likewise recommends the wing-low method even for its tricycle geared airplanes. The facts are that the slip required for the wing-low method is never as steep as the slips used for purposes of altitude dissipation, and is not steep enough to create a handling problem when used with flap settings of 20 degrees or less. This should alleviate the oft expressed concern over the use of the wing-down method in Cessna's.

Crossed-Controls

The idea of having the controls crossed while low and slow sends shivers down the spines of many pilots. Yet, this seems to be precisely what we are advocating when we recommend the wing-down method of crosswind correction. Are we wrong?

On close examination, an important consideration is that the extent of wing-down is not as extreme in fact as it appears when described in books or magazine articles. This means that, yes, the controls are crossed, but not excessively so. We are not on the edge of a cross-controlled stall until well into the flare, and by then the altitude is minimal. When the airplane does stall, the landing gear will contact the ground before any adverse gyrations can begin.

As reinforcement for the above, let's remember that a stall, any stall, is also scary and to be avoided, not just the crossed-control variety. Yet, this aversion to stalls has never prevented us from making three-point landings.

Hence, the answer to this apparent puzzle is that in a three-point landing, the stall (if it indeed occurs) will be so close to the ground that it will be inconsequential. But, if we are making a wheel landing, the wheels will indeed contact the ground while still at an airspeed that provides a significant margin above the stall. This same logic applies for crosswinds. And remember, that the pilot still has control of airspeed and power at his finger-tips even if the controls are crossed. Precise speed control remains as important here as for any other type of landing.

Given that these arguments convince the pilot of the merits of the wing-down crosswind correction, the apprehensions will gradually evaporate. But there is still one final card to be played, and that is the training exposure to the feel of crossed controls at altitude. The instructor can easily simulate the wing-down crosswind correction by having the student drop a wing during a normal descent and keep the airplane on a straight course with rudder. Air speed can be varied, different flap settings used, and the airplane flared to give the student the exact feel of the controls in the flare. Repetition of this maneuver at altitude will significantly alleviate the crossed-control concerns.

CRAB METHOD

On the surface, the crab method appears to be much simpler than the wing-down method. Using the crab technique, the pilot establishes a crab angle on final approach such as to keep the path of the airplane aligned with the runway in the face of the prevailing crosswind. As the approach progresses, the amount of crab is adjusted to compensate for the airplane's decrease in speed, and for the change in crosswind with the change in altitude. When the moment to touch down approaches, the pilot instantly applies a substantial amount of rudder to eliminate the crab at the instant of touchdown. It does sound simple, doesn't it?

A cursory examination of the advantages and disadvantages of the two methods leave us lukewarm in terms of deciding on which to use. The wing-down method offers the obvious disadvantage of passenger discomfort during a prolonged slip. In fact, "fear" is a more accurate word. Bear in mind, that the slip, to the uninitiated passenger, looks like a kamikaze run about to end in certain destruction. It also has the disadvantage of being difficult to execute in low wing aircraft with large wing spans. In this condition, it is difficult to judge the maximum allowable tilt without having a wing tip strike the ground. This of course is seldom a problem in light airplanes. The final disadvantage is that the method requires a bit more work on the part of the pilot because the corrections must be sustained over what may appear to be a lengthy period of time.

On the other hand, the main advantage of the wing-down method is that the most important item, namely the touchdown, is executed from a stable attitude properly aligned with the runway without drift. In addition, wheel landings and stall landings can be made with facility. This is of great importance to the taildragger pilot.

The crab type of landing has the distinct advantage of not scaring the passengers quite as much as the continuous slip, and it can be performed in long span airplanes without worry about dragging a wing tip. But the penalty is that it is a bit harder on the airplane.

Up to this point, we haven't discussed anything that hasn't been in print before. And the multitude of text books and magazine articles on the subject of crosswind landings generally leave the impression that one method is as good as the other so take your choice. The reader who believes all of this can stop reading at this point, choose his weapon, and fly off into the sunset (hoping that the crosswinds will not be too severe).

The problem is of course that most of these writers are parroting what they themselves had read the year before without giving the subject much thought. The truth of the matter is that the two methods discussed above are not equally safe when the type of airplane is taken in consideration. Since, from the beginning of these pages, our aim has been to write for the pilot of light general aviation airplanes, let's continue in that direction, with emphasis on taildraggers.

For the above category, the wing down method of crosswind landing is by far easier, safer, and more reliable than the crab technique. The reasons for this are quite clear.

In the first place, none of the scribes who claim that either method is good has ever explained to the author's satisfaction precisely how a pilot learns to kick out the crab at exactly the right moment. If the crab is removed a split second early, the airplane will begin drifting with the crosswind and will strike the ground in a crab. If this sounds like double talk, it isn't. Remember that the crab can only be kicked out for an instant, and an instant is a damnably short time span. On the other hand, if the crab is removed a split second too late, the airplane will touch down with a crab. Does this sound like "Catch 22"?

Let's examine Figures 7.1a and b for a moment. In Figure 7.1a, we see the flight path before the crab is removed. In Figure 7.1b, we have the flight path after the crab has been "removed" (assuming the airplane is still in the air). It certainly becomes obvious that the crab doesn't stay removed for long. After all, what rule of aerodynamics allows us to remove the crab in the first place? The answer is--none! It is only Newton's first law of motion which allows us to believe that we have this kind of control over the airplane.

Newton tells us that "an object in a state of uniform motion continues in that state of uniform motion unless acted upon by some outside force". In our case, the airplane, which in Figure 7.1a is on a flight path along the runway center line, will tend to continue on that same straight line when the rudder is kicked. However, immediately after the heading has been changed, the airplane will

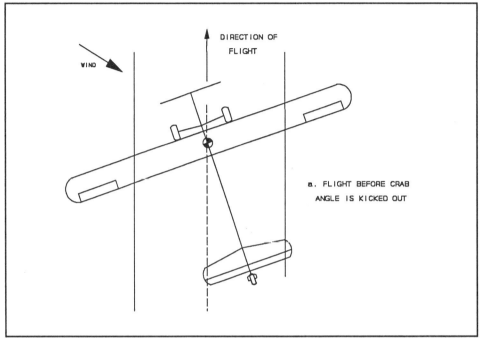

Figure 7.1a Taildragger in flight just before crab angle "kick-out"

take its new path, still with a crab. The "outside force" acting on the airplane is the crosswind component which will accelerate the airplane to the wind speed.

Some will argue that it takes time for this acceleration to take place. But, the time interval which they speak of is that required for the airplane's sideways velocity to reach the total value of the crosswind component. Generally forgotten is that in half that time interval, the airplane has reached roughly half the speed, and in many cases, this

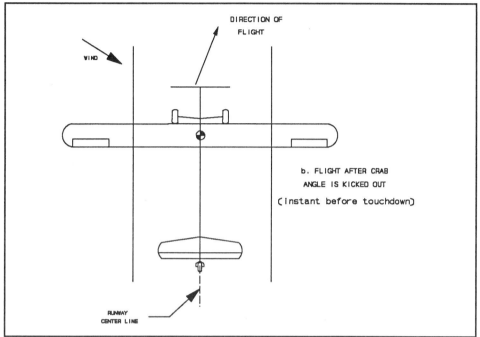

Figure 7.1b Taildragger after crab angle "kick-out"

certainly is not negligible. The true flight path of the airplane is shown in Figure 7.2. An analysis of the Crabbed Crosswind Landing is included in Appendix C.

In summary, it is almost impossible to exercise the timing required to make the "crab" method work reliably.

Of course, this begs the question " why is the method used so much if it is so poor"? And in cogitating an answer, we must consider that

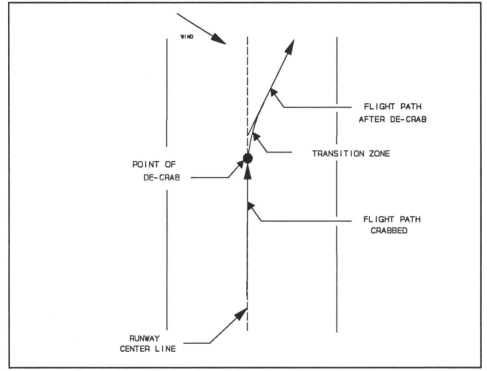

Figure 7.2 Timing of the de-crab maneuver

the method is used mainly in two types of airplanes, namely tricycle geared airplanes, or heavy airplanes.

In the case of the trike, the method works after a fashion simply because the geometry of the tricycle landing gear is so "forgiving" (see Chapter 3). In fact it is so forgiving that we see pilots landing them in crosswinds all day long without even attempting to use either method of crosswind landing compensation. Moreover, many of them don't even know that there is a crosswind blowing. If the tricycle geared airplane is of low wing design, the airplane is even more forgiving for two important reasons. First, low winged airplanes tend to have wider landing gear track making them more stable in the presence of a crosswind. Secondly, low wingers have a lower center of gravity (due to the wings and fuel tanks being closer to the ground), which benefits an airplane as much as it does a sports car.

In the case of a heavier airplane, the pilot may not have much choice as to which crosswind landing method to use, and indeed has a point in his favor if he does use the crab method. I say that he may not have a choice because his wing span may be so wide that he can't establish sufficient bank angle for the wing-down method without risking dragging a wing tip, an engine pod, or a fuel tank. The advantage he has is that, with a heavy airplane, the "instant" available to land the airplane after removing the crab angle is longer than for a light airplane. This is so because the wind will not accelerate a heavy mass as quickly as a light one (See Figure C-1 in appendix C). This is a fact well known to competition shooters in the really long range shooting matches. They all use heavy bullets to reduce the effects of wind drift on windy days. In addition, the heavy airplanes with their wing loading and large flaps generally don't exhibit the floating tendencies which a light airplane normally has. Hence, they can "get by" in this tricky situation because the airplane won't take as long in deciding to stall. In other words, the "instant" in which they are allowed to land is longer, and the time required is shorter. This combination at least helps.

At this point, the reader may be convinced that I'm against the "crab" method of crosswind landing, and he is right. The pilot of the light taildragger should become proficient at the wing down method and leave the crab method for the tricycle gear pilots.

Yet, I'm sure that I'll read at least one new magazine article per year glibly stating that either method is acceptable.

COMBINATION METHOD

Earlier in this chapter we mentioned the combination method briefly and then concentrated on the "wing-down" method. We now return to the combination method for some appropriate comments. First, since the combination method ends in a transition to the "wing-down" method as the flare is approached, it is also an acceptable method of crosswind landing. In evaluating which of the two methods should be recommended for use, the instructor is usually best guided by the student's level of experience. If the student is just beginning crosswind landings in the taildragger, the "wing-down" method will probably serve him better because the transition from crab to wing-down is eliminated. At this stage, the student doesn't need this additional complication. Likewise, his worry at this stage is a worry about a good landing and not a worry about passenger comfort. As the student gains experience with crosswind landings, the crab to wing-down transition can then be added, and the result is a more pleasing and professional product.

A final advantage of the combination method exists in the case of crosswinds of sufficient strength to tax the airplane's available control. Let's hypothesize a crosswind component of high enough velocity that the airplane lacks sufficient control travel to compensate for it with the wing down. And let's also stipulate that the crosswind component will decrease as the airplane loses altitude on final (this is often the case). The pilot may then compensate for the high crosswind component on final with a crab, since there is no limit to the amount of crab available. Then, when the airplane has descended to the runway—short final to flare—the transition to "wing-down" can be made in the crosswind of reduced intensity. And so we have the best of both worlds.

8

CROSS WIND LANDING GEAR

If we go back through the history of general aviation to the days just prior to World War II, we find that the available airplanes are largely equipped with conventional (taildragger) landing gear and suffer from the drawbacks which have been described in preceding chapters. These limitations, evidenced by the high rate of takeoff and landing accidents of the period, clearly showed that conventional gear was about to stymie the growth of general aviation. The key to further growth was to get rid of the conventional gear handicap and produce airplanes which would be less demanding of piloting skill and likewise less sensitive to the vagaries of the wind. Thus, utility would be dramatically increased, and flying would no longer be the domain of daredevils only. Everyone would be attracted to flying, and the airplane in its newfound utility would not have to be parked when the wind was brisk. So said the aeronautical cognoscente!

Used in the above sense, the word utility means putting the airplane into more hands, and more hands invariably means less capable pilots. There was no doubt that many of the leaders understood the handling difficulties spawned by the conventional undercarriage. There were also those of sufficient foresight who understood the need to make flying easier if more airplanes were to be sold. And when we say make "flying" easier, we generally mean make "take-offs and landings" easier, because here is where the bulk of light airplane accidents were (and still are) occurring.

It was also acknowledged that for real utility to be achieved, the airplane would have to be as useable as the family automobile. And very few people would be willing to interrupt their travels simply because the wind is blowing at 20 mph. and gusting to 30. Yet, it was not unusual in some parts of the country for light plane activity to just about cease during the windy hours of mid-day. This kind of limitation which often hindered the private pilot on a long trip also seriously impacted the cash register of the typical FBO who had to stop rental activities during similar time periods. Hence, the late 1930's was a fertile period for improvement of the light airplane, and the landing gear was to be the area in which investment would yield the greatest payoff. Thus, the coming years brought forth new developments in the form of tricycle landing gear, and conventional Cross Wind landing gear.

INTRODUCTION OF TRICYCLE LANDING GEAR

During this period, several individuals made their own contributions to solve the above problem. The most famous of these was Fred Weick who incorporated the tricycle landing gear on the Ercoupe which he was designing as a super-safe airplane. To be sure, the tricycle gear was not exactly "new". It had been used by Glenn Curtis as far back as the 1912 time frame. However, it had been dropped by airplane designers in favor of conventional (taildragger) landing gear for a number of years. While the tricycle gear was in some use during the 1930's, the airplanes so equipped (with one exception)

MAKE & MODEL	CERTIFICATION DATE	TOTAL QUANTITY PRODUCED
STEARMAN-HAMMOND Y-1-S	Jun '37	less than 20
WACO AVN-8 (& ZVN-8)	Apr '38	21
GWINN "AIRCAR" MODEL 1	May '38	3 ?
ERCOUPE 415-C	Mar '40	100 (6000 of the later 415-G model)
DOUGLAS DC-5	May '40	
GENERAL "SKYFARER" G1-80	Jul '41	12
CULVER "CADET" LAR-90 (including PQ-8/PQ-14)	Sep '41	8000

Table 8.1 Tricycle geared airplanes of the late 30's and early 40's

never reached large production volume during this period. These are listed in Table 8.1. The single exception to the small production quantities shown in Table 8.1 is the Culver PQ-8/PQ14 series which was built largely as "drones" for military use. This is a good example of the fragility of the taildragger having been recognized by the customer as well as by the designers. No one in his right mind would have considered the taildragger configuration for a drone due to the attrition rate which would result from any attempt to use these airplanes on windy days. The Ercoupe also reached large scale production, but did so only in its post WWII days.

Table 8.1 is not intended as a complete list of all tricycle geared airplanes of the era, but is presented to show the typical ones produced, and more importantly, the small quantities of the period.

The main reason why the designers had neglected the use of tricycle gear over the years was mainly due to questions of weight and drag. The design of an airplane is a great compromise of strength versus weight, where the additional weight of nose gear might eliminate most of the allowable baggage weight of the typical two-seater.

By the late 30's, the general aviation airplanes were becoming endowed with a bit more power, hence the weight and drag penalties of tricycle gear could be afforded if it would benefit sales. The accuracy of this statement is evidenced in the early postwar designs as embodied in the Beech "Bonanza", the North American "Navion", the Piper "Tri-Pacer", and the Cessna 172 marketed as soon as Cessna was able to read the proverbial hand-writing on the wall. Had Cessna stayed with the conventional geared 170 model, they would have lost the bulk of their sales to the above mentioned three.

To be sure, it is easy to criticize the concept of tricycle gear, and to suggest that since the tricycle gear pilot must still exert himself to add all the crosswind correction of the taildragger, why bother with this type of gear especially in view of weight and cost penalties. The answer is that it wasn't meant to be this way in the beginning. When Fred Weick was designing the Ercoupe with tricycle gear, his intention was that the pilot would be able to learn to fly this airplane more quickly because he would not have to learn about crosswind corrections. The intent was that the airplane would be flown to the ground with whatever amount of crab was required to fly a straight path along the runway center line, and would touch down with this crab or drift. Thus the brunt of the crosswind would be borne by the landing gear which had been designed of sufficient strength to be able to withstand this cruel punishment. Later tricycle gear were designed of lesser strength and therefore require crosswind compensation if the landing gear is to stay intact through a crosswind landing.

CROSS WIND GEAR

Cross Wind Landing gear, which was offered as an alternative to tricycle gear, was designed in the late 1940's and was sold for nearly as long as taildraggers were being built. This approach consists of installing castering mechanisms in the main landing gear of conventionally geared airplanes. The two types that were popular in the late 40's and early 50's were manufactured by Goodyear and sold under their brand name, and those designed by Geisse and manufactured by St Louis Machine Co.. Both types are still found in existence on classic taildraggers, with the bulk of those built having been installed on the Cessna 140, 170, 180, and 195 series. Many of these airplanes are still flying with their Cross Wind gear, while large numbers of them have been converted to the "straight" or non-castering conventional gear.

The basic principle behind the Cross Wind Gear is that the main landing gear (wheel) is mounted on a pivot allowing some amount of swivel (or caster) angle when the combination is acted upon by some side force. Some of the designs have a detent requiring that the side force exceed a threshold value before castering. This makes the airplane much easier to taxi. Other designs have a manually applied lock used for taxiing, with the gear unlocked for takeoffs and landings. The various designs generally include some damping, often in the form of friction, in order to prevent shimmy.

Before we discuss actual techniques to be used in flying the Cross Wind Gear, we must point out that not all pilots who have flown with this equipment have been enchanted with the exercise. An impromptu poll among pilots who have acquired some experience with Cross Wind Gear would most likely show that approximately 50 per cent of them love the gear, and the other half wouldn't have it as a gift. The latter are the pilots who will buy an airplane with Cross Wind Gear already installed and promptly have it replaced (at some significant expense) with the straight original non-castering wheels. Some of the time, this change is made before the owner has acquired enough experience with it to truly become comfortable. On other occasions, the owner has had no instruction on how to fly this brilliant invention, and succeeds in completely scaring himself in any of the several ways which we will discuss. That is the purpose of this chapter.

THE MECHANICS

First, let's look at the mechanics of the typical Cross Wind Gear. At least for the device made by Goodyear, the wheel was mounted to swivel about a king pin. To quote the report cited in Reference 3:

> " ...wheels had king pins, upon which the wheel castered, located within the wheels. The lower ends of the king pins were forward at 32 degrees when the airplane was in a three-point attitude.
>
> Cams arranged in conjunction with return springs were used to center the wheels when no side forces were applied and to compensate for a lowering of the axle due to angle of king pins, when the wheel castered from side to side. A spring loaded friction device was used to dampen out any tendency for the wheel to shimmy."

The referenced report goes on to state that tests were performed on the Piper J-3-C65 equipped with this first set of Cross Wind Gear in 90 degree crosswinds of up to 30 miles per hour. The only problem noted was some shimmy when the airplane was light on its landing gear, with the shimmy stopping when the full weight of the airplane was on the wheels. During later tests, the use of increased friction eliminated the shimmy altogether. It also states that in order to test the gear at high speeds, some landings were made at 90 mph. at the end of a dive. The wheels were able to caster 25 degrees to either side of the "straight ahead" direction. The quoted document is the Engineering report covering the flight test results of the first Goodyear Cross Wind Gear installed on the Piper J-3 used as a test vehicle.

A Goodyear house organ states that one year after the J-3 Cub tests (which were held in 1947), a Douglas DC-3 was equipped with Cross Wind Gear and flown, landing in 90 degree crosswinds of up to 45 mph. strength.

The above comment about the addition of friction material to reduce or eliminate shimmy should not be taken lightly. It can be a serious and aggravating problem.

As an example, picture the case of a pilot who has just bought the classic of his dreams (equipped with Cross Wind Gear), and during the next few flights discovers that his love has developed a terrible shimmy. His reaction will be to quickly take her in to the nearest mechanic and have the gear looked at. If the mechanic has no Cross Wind Gear experience, the result may well be that he will not discover that the friction pad is worn away, and won't replace the material. The owner flies it again, finds the same problem, and soon has the Cross Wind Gear removed and replaced with the original landing gear. Is it any wonder that so many owners have had their Cross Wind Gear removed?

The owner of any classic would do well to spend some time searching for the mechanic experienced in his particular breed with all of its idiosyncrasies. The Cessna 195 with Cross Wind Gear would be a good example.

Page 148

For practical purposes, all the pilot needs to know about the Cross Wind Gear itself is that it casters, and what are the limits between which do so. He also needs to know if the particular gear he's flying is lockable, and what are the circumstances under which it must be locked or unlocked. Finally, the pilot must have an awareness of what to look for when pre-flighting the gear.

The sketch in Figure 8.1 shows the castered position of the wheels (castered to the right side) in dashed lines. Remember that the wheels also caster to the other side.

DO'S AND DON'T'S OF FLYING CROSS WIND GEAR

In this Section, we will discuss how the Cross Wind Gear was intended to be used when it was originally designed, and then, we will look at some of the common errors and the penalties thereof.

LANDINGS

If we first look at Figure 8.2a, we see the airplane approaching at a decided crab angle with the wings level just as though the pilot were ready to make the transition to a side slip for the wing-low type of crosswind landing. Instead, the airplane remains in a crab, retains the wings level, and touches down in the crab without any crosswind compensation other than the crab itself. Figure 8.2b shows the airplane after touchdown. Notice that the wheels are now castered because of the side forces resulting from ground contact, and the airplane continues rolling out right down the center line. This is how the Cross Wind Gear was intended to be flown; no crosswind

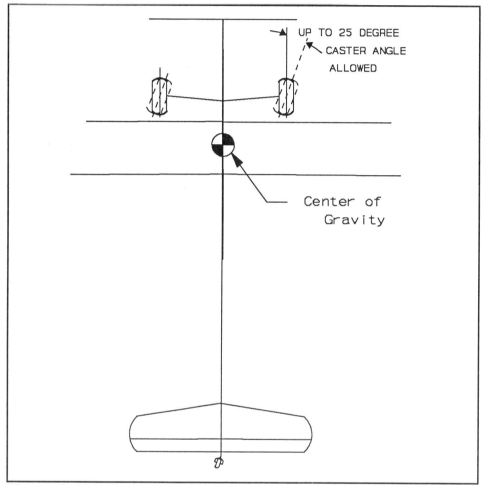

UP TO 25 DEGREE
CASTER ANGLE
ALLOWED

Center of
Gravity

Figure 8.1 Typical Cross Wind landing gear castered to the right

correction, wings level, fly it on with whatever crab angle is necessary to track down the center line. The type of landing to be made,

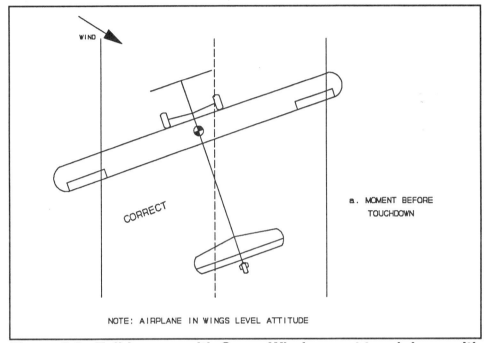

WIND

CORRECT

a. MOMENT BEFORE
   TOUCHDOWN

NOTE: AIRPLANE IN WINGS LEVEL ATTITUDE

Figure 8.2a Taildragger with Cross Wind gear at touchdown with crab—before

whether three-pointer or wheel landing, is left to the pilot's choice, as long either is made with the wings level.

When the landings are performed in this manner, and if the gear has been properly maintained, the Cross Wind Gear performs exactly as advertised.

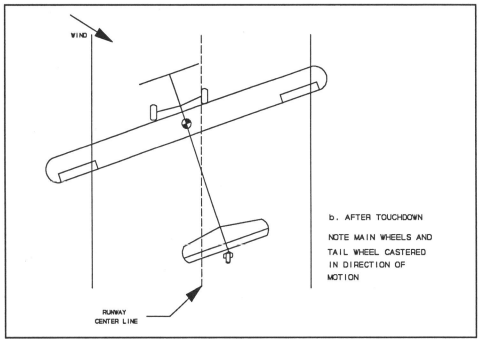

Figure 8.2b Taildragger with Cross Wind gear at touchdown with crab—after

TAKEOFFS

The takeoff with Cross Wind Gear is similar to the landings, with similar concerns, namely that the pilot have an awareness of if and when the gear is going to caster in the presence of a crosswind so as to prevent a sudden departure to the side. The pilot can prepare himself in one of the two following ways depending on the wind conditions.

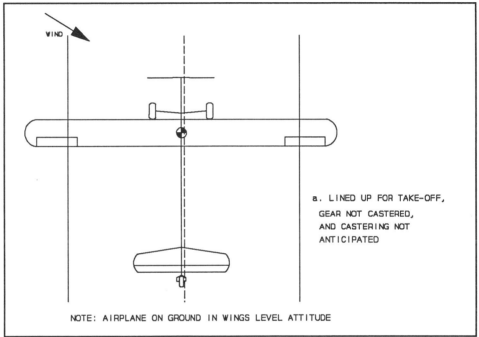

Figure 8.3a Taildragger with Cross Wind gear at takeoff

In the first case, we assume that the wind lacks sufficient strength to caster the gear as the pilot taxis into position for takeoff (on or slightly to the upwind side of the center line). He positions the airplane the same way he would if it possessed straight gear. This is shown in Figure 8.3a. As soon as power is applied for the takeoff and the airplane starts picking up speed, there is a great likelihood that the wheels will caster, hence the pilot must be ready for this, and make an immediate correction as shown in Figures 8.3b and 8.4.

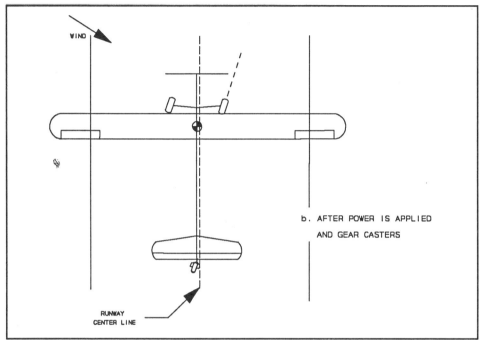

Figure 8.3b Taildragger with Cross Wind gear at takeoff

In the second case, the wind may have the strength to caster the gear as the pilot makes his line-up prior to takeoff. In such a scenario, the pilot would position the airplane as shown in Figure 8.5. He would then apply power, and would be reasonably assured that the airplane will track quite well down the runway.

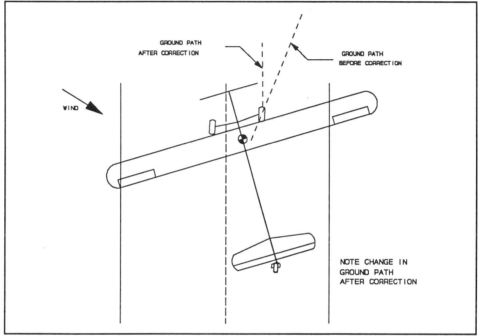

Figure 8.4 Taildragger with Cross Wind gear at takeoff—castering not anticipated

COMMON ERRORS

Let's now look at some of the common errors made by pilots who unfortunately haven't learned better. (Bear in mind that the only reason I can write about these errors is that I've made them all.) Perhaps the most common error is that which is typical of Cross Wind Gear pilots who haven't acquired much time on the gear, hence don't have much confidence in it or aren't comfortable with it. If we

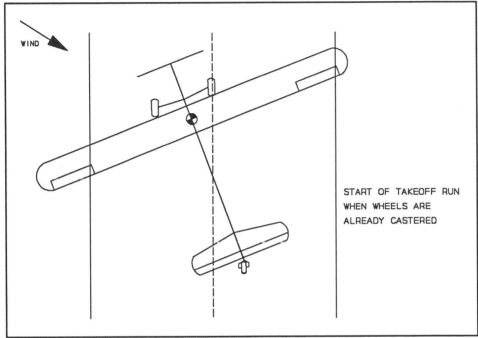

WIND

START OF TAKEOFF RUN
WHEN WHEELS ARE
ALREADY CASTERED

Figure 8.5 Taildragger with Cross Wind gear castered at takeoff

pick a day with a healthy crosswind, the pilot on final approach begins the mental argument of "should I land this thing in a crab as the procedure indicates", and who quickly decides "no, the crosswind is so strong that I'd better not take a chance on this Cross Wind Gear, so I'll land it like a regular taildragger with the wing-down method". The result is a disaster in the making, and if the pilot comes out of it without an accident, he is guaranteed to give up Cross Wind Gear faster than an emphysema patient gives up smoking.

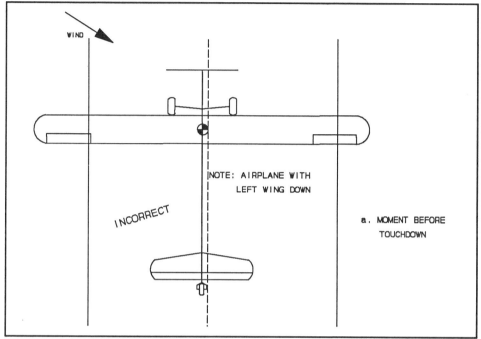

WIND

NOTE: AIRPLANE WITH
LEFT WING DOWN

INCORRECT

a. MOMENT BEFORE
TOUCHDOWN

Figure 8.6 Taildragger with Cross Wind gear landing—castering not anticipated

Let's look at Figures 8.6 through 8.10 to see what happens. In Figure 8.6, the airplane has not touched down yet, and has the left wing low due to the left crosswind. In Figure 8.7, the airplane has touched down on the left main wheel and the tail wheel, and is still traveling along the runway center line. So far, the crosswind technique exhibited is flawless. Now, as we look at Figure 8.8, we see the problem. In Figure 8.8, the airplane has settled on all three wheels and is now wings level. The crosswind still exists, and promptly

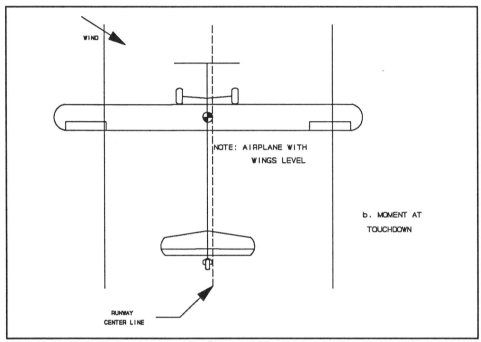

WIND

NOTE: AIRPLANE WITH
WINGS LEVEL

b. MOMENT AT
TOUCHDOWN

RUNWAY
CENTER LINE

Figure 8.7 Taildragger with Cross Wind gear after touching down without crab

exerts enough side force to caster the Cross Wind Gear. Hence, we see the airplane heading to the right at a rapid rate and closing on the runway lights in a manner which will elicit some unacceptable language.

Now, the scenario becomes even more exciting. Our intrepid pilot is now acutely aware of his predicament, and quickly cranks in a correction. Note, that salvation is to straighten out the airplane. In

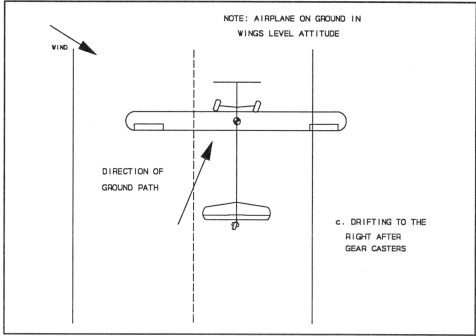

Figure 8.8 Taildragger with Cross Wind gear drifting to the right

order to do this, the pilot must turn sufficiently to the left such that the airplane will track parallel to the center line. However, let's not forget that the main wheels have castered giving the result shown in Figure 8.9. The wheels are now at a 25 degree angle with the center line, but the airplane is off the center line by some twenty or thirty feet, and the pilot now wakes up to the fact that while he's going to miss all the runway lights with the main landing gear, he's going to wipe them all out with the tail (if this is all happening on a narrow runway, it's already too late, and the accident is referred to in past

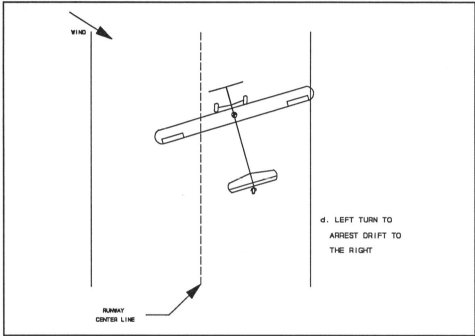

Figure 8.9 Taildragger with Cross Wind gear correcting to arrest right drift

tense) and promptly cranks in more left rudder in a last ditch maneuver to get back to the center line. This is shown in Figure 8.10 in which the tail is now even closer to the runway lights. If he is lucky and if the runway is wide enough, he will escape an accident, wonder what happened, curse Messrs. Goodyear and Geisse, and as soon as he's through flying for the day, will pour himself some strong refreshment. The above is not far-fetched, and has in fact happened to many pilots who have used Cross Wind Gear without benefit of

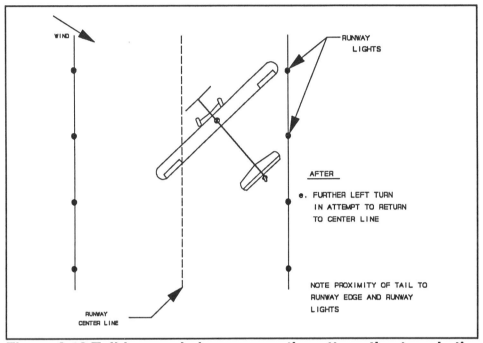

WIND

RUNWAY
LIGHTS

AFTER

e. FURTHER LEFT TURN
IN ATTEMPT TO RETURN
TO CENTER LINE

NOTE PROXIMITY OF TAIL TO
RUNWAY EDGE AND RUNWAY
LIGHTS

RUNWAY
CENTER LINE

Figure 8.10 Taildragger in large correction attempting to gain the center line

guidance. It is a likely reason for a pilot to develop a strong aversion bordering on hatred for the gear, and for him to promise himself to never own an airplane so-equipped.

This is an appropriate point to mention that the pilot should land slightly off the center line in the direction of the crosswind in order to give himself the maximum sea room. This is shown in Figure 8.11. In 8.11a, the pilot has used the normal technique of landing on the

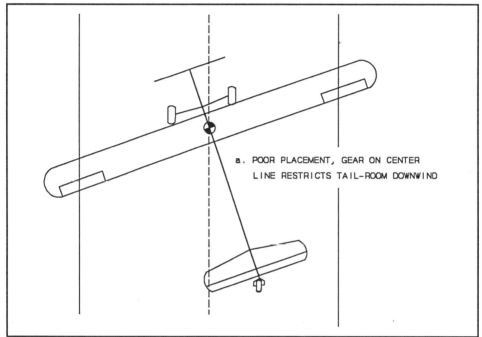

a. POOR PLACEMENT, GEAR ON CENTER LINE RESTRICTS TAIL-ROOM DOWNWIND

Figure 8.11a Landing on center line with Cross wind gear will restrict tail-space

center line. Note how much of the right hand side of the runway is used up by the fuselage and tail when the airplane is in a "castered" configuration. The pilot who lands slightly upwind of the center line, as shown in Figure 8.11b, will have much more maneuvering room.

We can summarize the takeoff and landing activity by stating that few problems are experienced by the pilot who flies the Cross Wind Landing Gear as it was intended to be flown. However, the pilot who

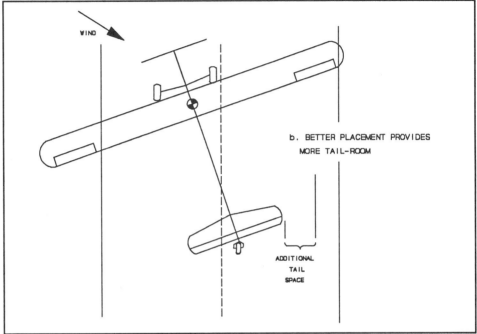

WIND

b. BETTER PLACEMENT PROVIDES
MORE TAIL-ROOM

ADDITIONAL
TAIL
SPACE

Figure 8.11b Landing with gear upwind of center line gives additional tail-space

distrusts the Cross Wind Gear and attempts to fly it in the manner of conventional landing gear will quickly create problems for himself.

TAXIING

Taxiing with the type of Cross Wind Gear which is not lockable can be a problem. The problem stems from two sources, namely the unpredictability of the gear and the narrow width of many taxiways at the smaller airports. If the winds are very light, and the Cross Wind Gear has been properly maintained and adjusted, the airplane will taxi like any other taildragger without the main gear castering. As the wind picks up in intensity however, there will be a threshold above which the gear will caster. What, then, does a pilot do if the wind is generally light and occasionally gusts above the threshold as the airplane is taxiing out. Curse a lot is the correct answer, because the pilot will have difficulty predicting if and/or when the gear will caster.

Figure 8.12 shows a typical scenario. In 8.12a, the airplane is taxiing in light winds and the gear has not castered. As the pilot approaches the intersecting taxiway and begins to make a left turn, the crosswind suddenly gusts to an intensity which casters the gear and drives it to the right uncomfortably close to the taxiway lights as shown in Figure 8.12b. Note the excursion which the pilot must now undertake if he is to complete the turn. However, the maneuver can only be performed if sufficient width remains on the taxiway. Otherwise, there is only one solution left, and that is to shut down the engine, move the airplane by hand to clear the lights and start the turn, and then re-start the engine and proceed. This is, to say the least, an embarrassing and humbling affair, one guaranteed to elicit strong language in the direction of Messrs. Goodyear and Geisse once again. How is this type of situation avoided? One way is to anticipate the possible, which, by the way, cannot always be done. Figure 8.12c shows how the pilot "might" have dealt with this situation. By anticipating the wind gusts and with a rough knowledge of the wind direction, the pilot could have cut the inside corner of his turn as closely as possible giving the tail maximum maneuvering room in case the gear should caster.

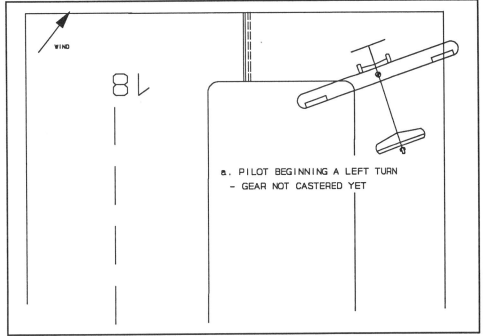

Figure 8.12a Taxiing turn—castering not anticipated

A second possibility is to use a technique often used by pilots of Cross Wind gear. This is to cause the castering of the gear through the use of brakes and the airplane's momentum. The thought behind this procedure is create the castering which is likely to come about anyway, but to do so at a predictable time rather than wait for "pot luck".

Much of this difficulty in predicting exactly what the gear would do under a certain set of circumstances is what helped give Cross Wind

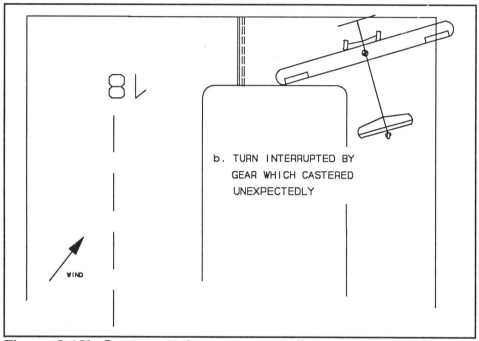

Figure 8.12b Gear castering unexpectedly creates diversion

Gear a bad name. Very simply, good pilots don't like the idea that the airplane just might not go where they've pointed it. This gives them the impression that the gear has a mind of its own and that they are not in control. If you now picture yourself taxiing a Cross Wind Gear equipped airplane the size of a deHavilland Beaver down some narrow taxiways in mid-winter when the taxiways are lined with 4 foot snow banks, and in the gusty winds associated with the passage of a cold front, you can sense the difficulties as you read this. Of course, the pilot who will have the most trouble with these

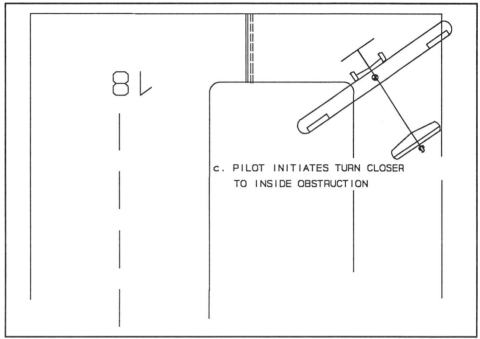

Figure 8.12c Cutting taxiing turn closer to obstruction provides increased maneuvering space

gymnastics is the one just transitioning from tricycle gear to taildraggers, primarily because he hasn't yet learned to keep the tail away from obstructions and is still of a mind that the tail (as in tricycle gear tail) will pass "over" the obstructions. The best solution to this problem, at least the taxiing portion of the problem, was invented by Goodyear and implemented in many of the Cross Wind Gear sold. This consists of a manually applied lock which, when engaged, kept the gear locked in a straight fore and aft alignment and prevented the wheels from castering.

LOCKED CROSS WIND GEAR

In order to alleviate the agonizing problem of taxiing with the gear kicking in and out of caster, Goodyear added a manual lock on some models. This lock consists of steel pins sliding in and out of a locking mechanism in each wheel, and flexible cables connecting the lock pins to a handle in the cockpit. The handle is usually located on the floor near the pilot's seat where it can easily be actuated with one hand. With this type of arrangement, the wheel castering mechanism is physically locked to prevent the wheels from castering during taxiing. Hence, the airplane with Cross Wind Gear locked taxies just like any other taildragger.

The procedure to use is as follows:

1. Pre-flight Inspection
    Check that the lock pins are engaged, appear straight and relatively free (to ensure that they will disengage when commanded).

2. Taxi
    While performing the pre-taxi check list, check that the Cross Wind Gear lock is engaged. Proceed to taxi in normal fashion.

3.   Takeoff
     Taxi the airplane onto the runway center line with the lock still engaged. Disengage the lock. Advance the throttle and expect the gear to caster as the airplane picks up speed and the wind provides side load. This will require a slight turn into the wind as shown in Figure 8.4.

4.   Pre-landing
     While performing the pre-landing check list, ensure that the gear lock is disengaged.

5.   Landing
     Perform a landing with the airplane crabbed into the wind in a wings level attitude.

6.   Post landing
     Bring the airplane to a stop on the runway, engage the gear lock, and in the initial taxiing, turn the airplane in a direction which will return the castered wheels to the neutral position. This will allow the lock pins to engage the lock mechanism. Taxi normally.

As the above shows, the lock mechanism takes much of the excitement out of taxiing with Cross Wind Gear, and eliminates all of the taxiing problems mentioned earlier. Of course, any new or additional device lends itself to the possibility of abuse, and this gear lock is not immune.

The potential pitfalls in the use of the lock are two-fold. First, there is the distinct possibility that the gear lock is accidentally engaged in flight. Considering that the lock pins are not heavy enough to survive the side loads accompanying landings in stiff crosswinds, landing with the gear locked will most probably damage the lock. It will either bend or break one or both of the lock pins. This eventuality can be guarded against by making the gear lock a pre-landing check list item, and then using the check list diligently.

The second pitfall is that there will be at least one pilot who believes that "the wind isn't very strong today, so I'll leave the gear locked for takeoff and landing". We've already discussed the results of such a mis-guided procedure, and will not repeat them here. The solution is to make sure through proper training and dissemination of information that all pilots flying the airplane are aware of the proper procedures. This is not necessarily easy to accomplish. For example, if it is a club owned airplane, and the club has a dozen or so pilots, Murphy's Law says that at least one pilot will not get the word. Also, if a new pilot joins the club, it is imperative that he be given a thorough ground indoctrination and check ride by the club's resident CFI or Check Pilot.

TILTED RUNWAY PROBLEM

A problem which is nonexistent for the pilot of conventional taildragger airplanes but which can cause Cross Wind Gear pilots a significant amount of grief is that of the tilted runway or tilted landing area if no particular runway is defined.

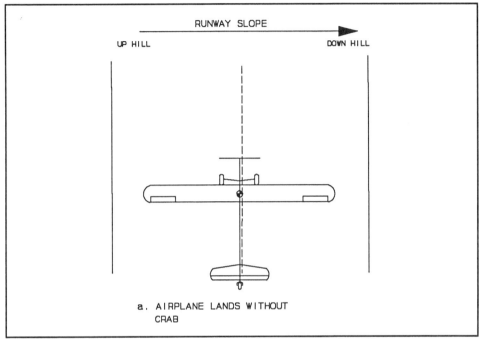

a. AIRPLANE LANDS WITHOUT CRAB

Figure 8.13a Airplane with Cross Wind gear landing on runway sloping to the right

Let's postulate a situation in which the runway in use is north-south, with east being in a slightly downhill direction. We will also specify that the wind is from the north right down the center line as shown in Figure 8.13a. Hence, no crosswind correction is required. If the pilot of an ordinary taildragger were landing to the north, the pitch of the runway would be generally ignored, and the pilot would make an ordinary approach and landing. Some time during the touchdown, the airplane would lean in the direction of the runway tilt, but that would not affect the roll-out appreciably.

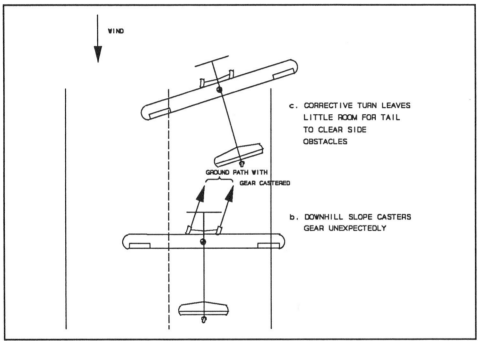

Figure 8.13b Downhill slope causes gear to caster unintentionally

In the case of an airplane with Cross Wind Gear, the airplane would normally be landed straight in along the center line and the pilot would be suddenly surprised to find that the pull of gravity towards the downhill side of the strip is sufficient to caster the main wheels in the downhill direction as we see in Figure 8.13b. As the airplane moves in that direction, the pilot discovers his proximity to the parallel ditch or other obstruction and applies a correction.

There are a couple of solutions to this problem. The first is to approach normally and apply a slight crab towards the uphill side just prior to touchdown. The resulting touchdown will give a path down the center line with perhaps a slight curve to the downhill side at the end of the ground roll. The second solution is simply to be aware before the landing that this is going to happen. Once aware, the pilot is prepared to give the airplane a quick rudder correction as he senses that the gear is about to caster. The anticipating pilot can also help himself by landing to the uphill side of the runway center line thereby leaving additional tail room. And, "No, you cannot lock the Cross Wind Gear manually before the landing" in order to avoid the problem.

IN GENERAL

On the average, the problems discussed above are problems only to the beginner totally inexperienced with Cross Wind Gear. The pilot who makes it a point to learn as much as he can from an experienced Cross Wind Gear pilot even before he climbs into the bird, and proceeds to learn gradually, and practices at an airport with decent runway and taxiway widths, will soon be quite comfortable with (and may even get to like) the gear and will wonder why I bothered to write this chapter.

When a pilot has difficulty with Cross Wind gear, the most common reason is that the castering of the gear occurs with a degree of uncertainty which is annoying to the pilot. Since the typical pilot feels more comfortable when in-charge of the airplane, a sudden castering of the gear and a departure of the taxiing airplane for a new direction is disconcerting in the extreme. Such behavior makes the pilot feel as though the airplane has acquired a mind of its own and will head for the bushes at the most crucial moment. This is how the gear gets its reputation for unpredictability.

In order to understand this uncertainty, the pilot must recognize that the castering is the result of side forces on the gear as the designer intended. And it is these side forces which are often unpredictable by the pilot who is inexperienced with the Cross Wind gear. This uncertainty is shown in Figure 8.12, where the gear doesn't caster until the airplane has started a turn which exposes the side of the fuselage to the wind, which, if of sufficient force will promptly cause castering. The difference between the beginner and the experienced pilot is that the beginner will be surprised. The experienced Cross Wind gear pilot will have anticipated the castering, allowed maneuvering space for it and will not be surprised. Hence, the beginner needs experience with the gear to learn when it will caster thereby reducing and eventually eliminating the element of surprise.

A simple maneuver which can make the beginner more comfortable with the gear is the 360 degree taxiing turn in each direction. These are performed where sufficient space exists to allow the tail to swing, and in the presence of winds of sufficient strength to cause the gear to caster. After a few such turns, the pilot will be able to anticipate castering and can then proceed with takeoffs and landings.

Once the pilot has become acclimated to the gear by practicing on the larger airports, he will find that he can then go on to the shorter and narrower fields without a problem.

9

TRANSITION PROGRAM

The transition from tricycle gear to taildragger can be an enjoyable experience when approached with a suitable attitude reflecting a desire to learn. This implies a willingness to listen and to complete enough practice to master the requisite skills. This is no time to be thinking in terms of 3 perfunctory takeoffs and landings and a sign-off.

Pilots desiring a transition program tend to fall into one of the following categories:

1. Pilots who are transitioning so that they can rent the taildragger in the future. These approach the program the way they approached their initial flight training. They will study what they are told to, and then train on a low pressure basis.

2. The pilot with a well filled logbook and a "just purchased" taildragger.

The pilot in the first case doesn't create a problem for the instructor. On the other hand, the second case is the source of migraines. If you picture the fellow as having spent weeks or months agonizing over the decision "to buy or not to buy," and having waited another month or two getting the maintenance of the machine and the ever present paper work straightened out, you see an individual without much patience left. The worse case scenario is the new owner who is convinced that he can fly the airplane without further instruction, and announces this to his chosen instructor adding "but my insurance company says that I've got to have 5 hours dual even though I know I won't need that much". He then wants to know why we can't do a couple of hours today and the rest tomorrow.

Fortunately, most of the transitioning pilots fit the first rather than the second category, and are the ones who make flight instruction a rewarding task. The client who avoids the temptation to pressure the instructor will be facilitating the entire process immensely, will minimize the risks involved, and, in the long run, will probably obtain much better training.

The result of a good program will leave both the pilot and the instructor with a glowing sense of accomplishment and pride. Let's proceed and see what a typical taildragger checkout or transition program might be like.

PROGRAM CONTENT

The introduction of the program to the prospective student should begin with a brief discussion of the student's background covering flight hours and equipment flown. If the training is to be conducted in student's own newly purchased taildragger, the instructor should be honest in assessing the difficulty factor of the airplane and communicating this to the student. Obviously, if the training is to be in a Cessna 185, the program will be substantially longer than if in a Champ or J-3 Cub.

The new FAR implemented on April 15, 1991 covering Taildragger instruction leaves little doubt as to what the level of proficiency must be at the end of the program (See FAR Par. 61.31 (g) in Appendix A). It does, however, leave to the individual instructor the means of getting there.

Assuming that the aspiring taildragger pilot already has previously obtained a Private or Commercial Pilot Certificate in tricycle geared airplanes, and that the pilot has no prior taildragger experience, the steps required follow.

GROUND SCHOOL

Transition to a new model should always begin with a ground school session addressing all of the following, most of which can be taken from the Pilot's Operating Handbook (except for empty weight and C.G. data):

- Fuel System

- Weight & Balance

- V speeds

- Limitations

- Performance—Fuel consumption, Engine operation parameters

- Emergency procedures

- Restrictions that haven't been covered in any of the above.

Most of these items can be covered rather quickly unless the airplane is a recent acquisition for which the instructor will require additional time for his own familiarization. Once this has been covered, we can move on to the taildragger specific subjects which include

- Torque sources and their control

- Positioning of controls for taxiing

- Normal takeoffs and landings

- Wheel landings

- Crosswind takeoffs and landings

- Operation of any unusual or special equipment, such as Cross Wind gear, locking tailwheel, etc..

- Recovery from a bounce

The total ground school material can be covered in 2 hours if the airplane is a familiar model, with additional time being required to address any strange items. It is also possible to cover some of the ground school as part of the pre-flight briefing if the instructor will successfully fight off the temptation to "rush it" in order get in the air quickly. Indeed, the various explanations may be more effective if given or repeated just before practice in the airplane.

FLIGHT PROGRAM

The flight lessons are grouped in Blocks of items to be accomplished, with the intent that the blocks be performed in the sequence listed whenever possible. Each block will consist of one or more flights.

Block 1
We begin with taxiing, demonstrate a normal takeoff, let the student fly the climb to the practice area, and familiarize himself with the airplane by performing turns, a stall series, slow flight, and a some simulated patterns ending in a go-around. If time permits, ground reference maneuvers may be performed to increase the pilot's comfort in the airplane. Then, the instructor will demonstrate a normal (three-point) landing.

Block 2
Beginning in rather benign wind conditions, normal takeoffs and landings are performed. This work can all be in the pattern unless the student exhibits difficulty with speed control or coordination. In such a case, the instructor should revert to simulated patterns at altitude until the deficiency has been resolved. Recovery from the bounce should also be covered here. Winds should be light, (under 6 knots) or if stronger, should be aligned with the runway.

Block 3
We have now reached the point for crosswind takeoffs and landings. The crosswind component should be limited to 6 or 8 knots.

Block 4
Wheel landings are performed, with winds as specified in Block 2.

Block 5
Crosswind operations with the crosswind component from 10 knots and increasing progressively to the airplane's maximum allowable value are the order for this block. The landings will undoubtedly be wheel landings.

All blocks should include emergency procedures, and must be bracketed by pre-flight and post-flight briefings.

Some comments are in order regarding the order of the Blocks of instruction. Remembering that "the best laid plans of mice and men........" will often be rendered askew by unexpected conditions, it may become necessary to change the order somewhat. For example, Block 4 may well precede block 3, and Block 3 may supersede Block 2, although this will make life more exciting for the instructor.

PROGRAM LENGTH.

Recognizing that we cannot make a solid commitment on the time which will be required for the above program, we can mention typical time averages which are useful as a starting point for discussion.

Block Number	Flight Time Required (hours)
1	1.5
2	2.0
3	2.0
4	2.5
5	2.5
Total	10.50

Table 9.1 Length of typical taildragger transition program

These are shown in Table 9.1, and must be interpreted as minimum. In some cases, 15 to 20 hours may be needed before the transitioning pilot is safe for crosswind operations with passengers.

The issue of solo time is guaranteed to become a sticky item, mainly because the FAA has made no provision for solo practice prior to the final sign-off if the pilot already has a Recreational, Private or Commercial certificate.

Prior to the promulgation of FAR 61.31(g), a Flight Instructor could legally turn lose a student for some solo practice of the various maneuvers listed in this program. This was usually beneficial, and saved the pilot some money. This was generally followed by some additional dual or a final check ride to verify proficiency, after which the instructor would sign-off the student.

The advent of the new regulation just mentioned no longer allows this practice. Since the pilot already has a Recreational or higher pilot certificate, his time can only be logged as Dual or Pilot In Command, and PIC time may not be logged in taildraggers prior to the logbook endorsement. Yet, if the pilot is the holder of a Student Certificate, the instructor can legally sign him off for solo in the model of airplane for a 90 day period. This is an interesting state of affairs, to say the least.

HIGH SPEED TAXIING

The reader will perhaps have noticed that the subject of High-Speed Taxiing has not been introduced as a training maneuver. The reason for this is not that the author has forgotten to include it, but rather that the discussion of this subject was reserved for special treatment. (The mechanics and dangers of high speed taxiing have been discussed in chapter 4). High speed taxiing is often suggested, and even recommended by many pilots as a training maneuver for the pilot transitioning to taildraggers. This advice is usually given in complete ignorance of the realities. Those recommending the maneuver usually are not instructors, or if they are, they have no prior experience in taildragger transition work.

The facts are that the high speed taxi maneuver subjects the pilot and the airplane to unnecessary risks for an unacceptable length of time. The maneuver is difficult even for an experienced taildragger pilot and is seldom used as an ordinary maneuver in normal practice except when a long taxi needs to be expedited, in which case the maneuver is best left to experienced taildragger pilots and not to beginners. During high speed taxiing, the exposure to the risk of an accident is probably ten times greater than for ordinary takeoff and landing practice. And, when people suggest it as a training maneuver prior to takeoffs and landings, they have the order of operations wrong. They should be recommending takeoffs and landings as practice for high-speed taxiing because that sequence makes more sense.

When a pilot is learning torque control by practicing consecutive takeoffs and landings, the exposure to the dangers inherent in loss of control is relatively short, and control generally improves bit by bit with each subsequent takeoff. If there should be a slight loss of control, the instructor is usually able to salvage the situation by lifting the airplane off the ground away from the runway lights and other hazards (if sufficient airspeed was being gained at the time). Likewise, during a practice wheel landing, the airplane is kept on the mains with the tail elevated for a relatively short time. As the pilot tries to keep the tail in the air, the tail is continuously descending due to the power having been retarded.

During a high speed taxi maneuver, we find that the maneuver is neither fish nor fowl. The pilot is not trying a takeoff (which would quickly get him away from the dangers surrounding him) nor is he making a landing which would take a relatively short time. In fact, he is attempting to prolong a dangerous situation (airplane on the mains with half to three-quarters throttle), and with little to be gained. The airplane doesn't really want to stay on the ground because too much power is applied, and the pilot doesn't really want it to fly because he is practicing taxiing. But if he relaxes just slightly, the tail may descend just a bit thereby creating just enough angle of attack for the bird to fly off. And now, he has a real problem. The airplane is unexpectedly in the air—barely flying—with half or so throttle. If the pilot is smart enough, he will quickly but smoothly apply full throttle and depart the scene to return for a landing at a time of his choosing. If he does anything else at this stage, he is poised on the edge of disaster. If he does nothing, he will soon run out of runway and probably encounter an inadvertent stall. On the other hand, if he attempts to land it from this position, he may botch it and wipe out the airplane. In fact, if he is capable of landing without mishap from this attitude and altitude, he did not need this practice taxiing in the first place. Hence our contention that this is a useless maneuver with excessive risk.

Many taildraggers have been literally destroyed in this manner, and the next person to recommend this as a training maneuver should be made to pay the insurance premium on the airplane in question.

TAILDRAGGER INSTRUCTOR

The task of the Certificated Flight Instructor has always been and continues to be a difficult one. The purpose of this chapter is to provide some guidance and assistance to the beginning taildragger instructor with the intent of making his job a bit easier and possibly safer. This advice may also be of interest to the experienced instructor who doesn't need it as much as the beginner since he has already learned it all, the hard way.

FLIGHT INSTRUCTOR BACKGROUND AND PREPARATION

From the first moment the flight instructor thinks of instructing in taildraggers, it is very important for a number of reasons that he make some basic decisions about what he believes his minimum qualification should be before he sallies forth.

If the instructor is a typical case, we can easily guess that his aviation background is similar to the following:

> He earned his CFI in the common tricycle geared airplanes within the last year or two, has accumulated a few hundred hours of instruction time, and has taken a shine to a locally

available Citabria. He soon obtains a check-out in the little taildragger, and after five or six hours of solo time, he is suddenly asked to "checkout so and so" because the regular instructor who usually dispenses the Citabria dual has now left town to fly for the airlines.

This is a strong temptation which should be avoided with a strength akin to the vows of priesthood for several good reasons.

First on the list of reasons for foregoing the above opportunity is the question of "How good was the instructor's check-out in the airplane in the first place"? If he had received a thorough and professionally developed checkout program from a highly experienced taildragger instructor who was able to provide ground school as well as flight instruction (and emphasis here should be on the "thorough"), he is an exceptional case and ahead of the game. His next question then is on recency of experience. And the answer depends on whether he is worrying about legal considerations or common sense. In order to teach in taildraggers our instructor (assuming he holds an unexpired Instructor Certificate with the Airplane-Single Engine rating) needs no more than three takeoffs and three landings to a full stop in a taildragger in the preceding ninety days. See excerpt from FAR 61.57 subparagraph (c) in Appendix A. While this meets the legal requirement, it is a far cry from what common sense should dictate. But let's move on and come back to this question later.

The more serious problem at the moment is if the instructor is not an exceptional case in terms of his own taildragger checkout. What if he never received more than an hour or two in the airplane, and this from a non-instructor. Or, heaven forbid, has he simply checked himself out without benefit of formal instruction from an experienced instructor. If either of these is indeed the case, our instructor needs a lot more than three takeoffs and landings. But how much time does he really need?

While there is no clear cut school answer to the above question, we can probably arrive at an acceptable and viable one rather quickly by reviewing a bit of history. First, remember that most of the flight instructor requirements were originally established by the CAA in the pre WW-II era when all pilots were taking all their training in taildraggers (except for the seaplane pilots of course). If we picture the total 200 hours required for the instructor certificate as having been in taildraggers, and ask how much of that time was spent in the takeoff and landing phase, we would probably conclude that one fifth of the 200 hours, or 40 hours were actually spent in T.O.'s and landings. Hence, if our instructor accumulates 40 hours devoted to taildragger takeoffs and landings, he will have reached the experience level which the typical instructor who had done all of his flying in taildraggers would have. This I believe to be an acceptable experience level for an instructor to begin teaching in taildraggers, provided that a significant percentage of it has been in some demanding wind conditions. The important point here is not the amount of time logged per se, but the variety of experience, the difficulty level, and the amount learned from all this. The instructor cannot teach what he doesn't know, nor can he accurately judge what he has not experienced. Of course, if our instructor is planning to teach in a Part 141 environment, his requirements are likely to be established for him by the Chief Flight Instructor of the establishment.

Once the minimum experience requirement is met, the taildragger instructor faces the constant need to remain current, and this may be a bit more difficult to do than for the tricycle gear instructor especially if there are relatively few taildragger airplanes available at his location. Currency and proficiency are difficult to maintain when the taildragger is only available and flown occasionally.

A second potential pitfall will present itself when the instructor is asked to give dual in a taildragger model which he has never flown. The attraction of a new airplane is always great, and there is a great temptation for the instructor to believe that he can "handle it" because "it's just another airplane". To go ahead on this basis would in most cases be courting disaster. As a minimum, the instructor needs a checkout from someone experienced in the breed, and also needs sufficient pilot in command time to have sampled how the airplane needs to be handled in crosswinds. Any less is sheer lunacy.

The taildragger instructor must develop an awareness for his limitations based on his experience. For example, an instructor with 3,000 hours total time in tricycle gear and with 12 hours P.I.C. time in Citabrias must understand that his judgment and his handling ability with respect to the takeoff and landing scenario is more likely to be 12 hour ability rather than a 3,000 hour skill level. This is the primary reason why the FAA requires that the instructor applying for an additional flight instructor rating must:

"..have had at least 15 hours as pilot in command in the category and class of aircraft appropriate to the rating sought."[1]

We don't mean to imply that FAR 61.191 applies to the taildragger instructor although it perhaps should, but the logic behind it certainly applies. A nearly identical situation faces the flight instructor with a brand new "single engine sea" rating.

Finally, it is highly recommended that the instructor strive to learn as much as possible about the taildraggers which we have left. Much can be gained by reading and absorbing the Pilot's Operating Handbooks and the numerous Check Flight articles appearing in the popular aviation magazines provided the reader is judicious enough to not believe everything in print.

Given that the instructor is convinced as to his ability and understands his limitations, we are ready to discuss his forthcoming relationship and responsibilities towards his students.

RESPONSIBILITIES

The taildragger instructor, like any other flight instructor has the responsibility to teach, with the added stipulation that he must prevent the student from damaging the airplane and injuring the occupants. Granted that the student may learn a great deal from a crash, our society including the FAA, insurance companies, and peer

---

[1] See FAR subparagraph 61.191(b) reproduced in Appendix A.

flight instructors not to mention the student and the management does not accept it as a training method. (The fact that it works as a training tool is well documented by the number of automobile accidents which young drivers have within the first year or two after issuance of their initial driver's license).

Nevertheless, the instructor must allow the student some latitude to make mistakes during the learning process, but must also execute the "save" maneuver in order to prevent accidents. He must also serve as the student's guardian for those training flights when he won't be aboard the airplane. Hence, he is the watchdog over the weather and the maintenance state of the aircraft.

In discussing weather as it applies to taildragger training, our comments will be restricted to wind conditions since the other weather questions remain the same as for tricycle gear pilots. But an awareness of wind and its effect is crucial to taildragger instruction.

The first consideration is to conduct the first training flights in rather benign conditions if the student is to gain any experience at the controls during takeoff and landing. A crosswind at this time will probably force the instructor to handle the controls himself in order to prevent a disaster. As the student gains experience, and by way of having demonstrated them, appears to understand the normal takeoff and landing, he should be introduced to light crosswinds prior to progressing to more demanding conditions.

Crosswind components exceeding 10 knots and approaching the airplane's maximum allowed value may tax the instructor's skill and judgement, but are too important to be omitted. The transitioning pilot has a right to expect this level of training—at the proper time—and without it, will be forced to learn it on his own. The difficulty for the instructor is the exercise of judgement which will separate wind conditions which are "excellent for training" from those which would be "foolish to attempt training in". This judgement will also depend on the student's ability level.

The use of grass to initiate crosswind training is a good means of making the process easier and safer. Grass is forgiving, yet will still allow the student to notice errors made with less risk to the equipment. But, for operations to be conducted safely, it is imperative that the grass surface be personally checked by the instructor to ensure the absence of debris, holes, rocks and tall grass which might not be visible from the air. On the other hand, if all the taildragger training has been conducted on grass, the program isn't considered complete until crosswind experience has been obtained on paved runways.

We will digress slightly to point out that the instructor's association with his taildragger student is likely to be much shorter than it is with a normal student. The relationship with a normal student is that the instructor provides 10 to 15 hours of dual before the student starts solo work. We then have the periodic phase checks, and the cross country dual to later be capped off with night dual and the final training leading to the recommendation ride. This total contact can easily span some 60 to 80 flight hours over many months. The taildragger transition student, however, is a different case. If the pilot already possesses a private pilot certificate and owns the taildragger in question, he may come to you with the best of intentions, yet, pressure the instructor into a premature sign-off in three or four flight hours. At best, the instructor won't spend more than 12 to 15 hours with the typical taildragger transition student. The consequences of this potentially short relationship is that the instructor will not get to know the student as well, and will find it more difficult to assess the student's judgement.

The maintenance state of the airplane is the instructor's next concern. And while he should be concerned with the maintenance of the entire airplane, as any instructor should, we need to emphasize that the brakes must be in top form. This means from both seats if the airplane is equipped with dual sets of brake pedals. As mentioned earlier, the instructor is responsible for "saving" the airplane from potential accidents. And in order to accomplish this, the brakes, rudder and throttle will be the most often used tools for this purpose. A suddenly developing ground loop to the left cannot be arrested by the instructor if the right brake master cylinder "should have been topped off" before the flight. Instructional flights should not be undertaken with malfunctioning equipment for three good reasons:

1. It is illegal.

2. It is an unnecessary handicap for the pilot and instructor, and can lead to an accident.

3. It is a demonstration of poor judgment to the student who has a right to expect better of the instructor and it encourages the formation of poor habits.

Airplanes with deficiencies rendering them of questionable airworthiness may still be flown, if a ferry permit has been issued by your local FAA GADO or FSDO for that flight. However, the regulations governing use of the airplane under a ferry permit preclude its use for dual instruction.

Additional information on specific maintenance items of importance to taildraggers is provided in the MAINTENANCE section of Chapter 11.

In a similar vein, the subject of fully functioning dual controls needs to be aired. The requirement for dual controls is spelled out in FAR subparagraph 91.21 (see Appendix A) and makes it clear that it is a requirement for dual instruction. While allowances are made for the use of a throw-over control wheel, note that it is only allowed for "instrument instruction". Again, don't succumb to pressure to give dual with such a rig. It is illegal.

WHEEL LANDINGS

No maneuver in basic VFR flying is as poorly understood as the wheel landing. Yet, the wheel landing is vital to the taildragger pilot's safety. Without the knowledge, experience, or skill to perform this maneuver, the pilot severely limits the use of his taildragger to relatively benign wind conditions. He also endangers the lives of his passengers if, in such ignorance, he ventures forth in conditions which will give him 90 degree crosswinds in the 12 gusting to 18 knot range.

Yet, nothing mentioned in the above paragraph will assist the instructor in teaching this maneuver, which I firmly believe is the item in VFR flying which is the most difficult to teach. While Chapter 6 contains the mechanics of <u>how to perform</u> the maneuver, this section is intended as advice to the flight instructor on the specifics of <u>how to teach</u> wheel landings.

As for any other maneuver, the first introduction should be at the blackboard where a thorough explanation of objectives and procedures is given and questions are answered. Only then should the instruction proceed in the airplane.

The easiest manner in which to approach the maneuver is to not attempt a landing on the first two or three passes, but to simply plan to roll the main wheels on the surface for a short distance and then apply power for an immediate takeoff. It is best performed at higher than normal landing speeds, and with flaps up. In this configuration, the tail never touches the ground, the throttle is never retarded all the way to idle, and to the beginner, the maneuver appears simple. Tell the beginning taildragger pilot that "we're going to do wheel landings next", and he will cringe and crank up his pucker factor to 10. But tell the same individual that "we're not going to land, but we will gently roll the wheels on the runway and leave", and he thinks that "this is going to be fun". The technique here is to approach in an attitude which will result in the mains just "kissing" the runway. In other words, contact is from a grazing flight path with very little vertical velocity. This makes the maneuver easier. It is best performed where the runway length is more than adequate. In this way, the pilot will not be tempted to rush, and will give a better performance.

After this rolling maneuver is performed successfully, the instructor can then pick up the pace by informing the pilot that on the next pass, the instructor will retard the throttle to idle (after the rolling has been established) and that the pilot is expected to maintain the tail in the elevated position by continuous and ever increasing amounts of down elevator (forward stick) as speed is dissipated.

Once this is successful, the germ has been planted for good wheel landings, and the pilot can go on to improvements such as the use of less power and speed, use of flaps, wheel landings on grass fields, and finally, wheel landings in crosswinds of high enough intensity to require a touch-down on one wheel.

It is important for the pilot to realize that the wheel landings skills built up through the above procedure will quickly fade if not reinforced through some fairly intensive practice. One way of encourageing that type of practice is for the pilot to arbitrarily decide to make all his landings as wheel landings for the next few hours, and then alternate from wheel landings to three-pointers for every other landing.

FINAL ADVICE TO THE INSTRUCTOR

Don't let undue pressure from a student bend your judgment of flight conditions for dual instruction. The student is always in a hurry and anxious to fly, and he initially will not understand why you are unwilling to take him out in a 15 knot crosswind while he swears that he can fly a Cessna 152 in 20 knots without a problem. It is your job to make him understand the reasons, bearing in mind that you must also teach him judgment. If he doesn't learn it from you, he will have to learn it on his own, albeit more expensively perhaps.

Proceed slowly with the transitioning pilot's logbook endorsement. Make sure that crosswind proficiency has been demonstrated to your satisfaction in conditions which preclude good landings being the result of sheer luck. Remember that you are the final judge. Since the pilot already has a pilot's certificate, his proficiency is not going to be reviewed by an examiner.

Be aware that the depth of technical learning which the student is willing to accept in ground school will vary from student to student. Not all will express a willingness to sit through an explanation of the torque curves of Chapter 5. Indeed, very few will! So be it. There is nothing illegal about letting students learn torque control the hard way as long as it is done safely. But it will take longer.

Do convince the student that the high amount of time which he has logged in other airplanes doesn't contribute much weight to his judgement and skill in handling a taildragger for takeoffs and landings. Our earlier discussion of this matter as it applies to instructor time and experience is every bit as applicable here.

Do make the student aware of possible emergency conditions and provide tips as to how to cope with them. For example, a failed brake need not be catastrophic if the student knows that the airplane can be successfully stopped by using the remaining usable brake in a pumping motion with opposite rudder applied to prevent a swerve. It will also help if the landing is made on the same side of the runway center line as the failed brake. Taxiing can be successfully negotiated by keeping the turns wide enough to keep the tail wheel within the steerable range. It will help even more to practice a simulated failure. Likewise, the possibility of bungee failures in airplanes with Piper J-3 style landing gear should be discussed. Granted that for a neophyte taildragger pilot to see his right or left gear leg hanging at a strange angle will be a traumatic experience, it is guaranteed to be much worse if his instructor has never discussed the possibility with him nor the recommended action.

Don't forget to keep track of the taildragger pilots whom you have checked out, and don't hesitate to recommend additional training anytime their observed performance is found wanting. Remember that your advice may exert more influence than you might think. There are some pilots who don't solicit dual on their own after they've received their checkout or license. However, these same people may follow through with the instructor's suggestion of "I think you and I should go up for a couple sessions of crosswind work". The pilot now has an excuse to obtain additional dual on the basis that "my instructor made me". Whatever the rationalization, the fact that the instructor convinced the pilot to get the dual is positive. Don't ever be bashful about using this ploy. You may prevent an accident that way.

Do maintain high standards for your flying, and maintain high expectations for the flying performance and professionalism of your students. And by no means should you keep the fact a secret that, since they've obtained their instruction from the best instructor, they should be the best pilots. It will give them a goal to shoot for.

Finally, don't hesitate to point out to the aspiring taildragger pilot that he can do much to help himself get ready for taildragger flying while still in tricycle geared equipment. And this involves skill in crosswind takeoffs and landings. Remember that the principles of drift cancellation are the same for both types of airplane. Until the airplane touches down, it doesn't know what type of landing gear it has. Hence, good crosswind correction habits developed in tricycle geared equipment will make a subsequent taildragger transition so much easier, shorter, and less expensive.

IMPORTANT REGULATION CHANGE

Effective April 15, 1991, subparagraph (g) requiring an instructor's endorsement for flight in a taildragger was added to FAR 61.31. This new regulation now neatly places transitioning pilots in one of two categories and has some effect on the conduct of the training program. At issue is the question of whether or not the pilot can be allowed solo practice prior to completion of the taildragger checkout.

Lets look at the 2 categories.

1. Pilot holds a valid Student Pilot Certificate

2. Pilot is the holder of a Recreational, Private, or Commercial certificate.

In the first case, the student may solo at the instructor's discretion provided that the instructor suitably endorsed the student's certificate and logbook. Note that the instructor may stipulate weather conditions covering the allowed solo. For example, an endorsement limiting the solo flights to crosswind components of less than 10 knots is one way to allow solo practice in conditions considered safe for that student.

But if your "student" is from category 2 above, and has not logged PIC time in taildraggers prior to April 15, 1991, there are no provisions in the regulation allowing solo practice in taildraggers prior to the flight instructor's endorsement. This means that the only time the transitioning pilot can fly the taildragger without the instructor on board is after the logbook has been endorsed stating that the objectives listed in FAR 61.31 (g) have been met. This is the FAA's official interpretation of that regulation at this time.

11

ODDS AND ENDS

A thorough taildragger background for the prospective pilot or instructor should include a great deal of material which is not generally taught in formal courses. This material is what one might term "taildragger lore", and years ago might have been acquired by hanging around the airport and listening to people willing to share their knowledge and experiences. Alas, in this day of liability, this practice is discouraged and the interested must acquire the knowledge elsewhere. The purpose of this chapter then is to share some of these points, and perhaps more importantly, to encourage the curiosity which will lead to the acquisition of additional "nuggets".

TAILDRAGGER CHARACTERISTICS

There are a number of important characteristics which contribute to ease or anguish in taildragger handling. Some of these will be discussed here in general terms, with others specific to a particular breed.

CENTER OF GRAVITY LOCATION

The location of the airplane's Center of Gravity (C.G.) with respect to the main landing gear is a case in point. With the C.G. located relatively far aft of the landing gear, the airplane will be less stable in the face of touchdown with some drift. This location of the C.G. increases the airplane's angular momentum about the vertical axis and makes it more difficult to stop the motion of a ground loop because more corrective control is required. The Cessna L-19 Bird Dog is a good example.

Taildraggers which have the C.G. relatively close to the main gear tend to be more stable with respect to ground loops, but have a tendency to nose over more easily with sudden or excessive use of brakes. The Luscombe Silvaire series is an example, as well as is the Cessna 140 series. In fact, this problem has been solved in many of the 140's in existence by the addition of permanent wheel extensions. These move the wheels slightly forward and increase the distance from main wheels to C.G.. Of course, based on our earlier discussion, the price of the modification is an increase in the tendency to transform drift at touchdown into a ground loop.

Another oft forgotten consideration with respect to C.G. is the height of C.G. above the wheels. While low wing taildraggers tend to have lower C.G.'s than their high-wing brothers, and therefore slightly more stability on the ground, there is some variation between the various high wingers. For example, the Cessna series of work horses, the Cessna 180 and 185 all carry most of their fuel in wing tanks, hence will sport a higher C.G. when full of fuel, with the C.G. gradually being lowered as fuel is consumed. This is common among high wing airplanes, but is the exact opposite condition from the deHavilland DHC-2 Beaver. These, without range extending wing tip tanks, carry all their fuel in belly tanks beneath the cabin floor. Hence, they are at their lowest C.G. condition when heaviest with fuel, and the C.G. rises with fuel burn. Of course, there are some pilots who would treat this matter of C.G. location as trivial information and not worthy of mention. However, the author believes that a pilot should know as much of the characteristics of the airplane which he is flying as possible.

Another instance of C.G. location being different in different models of a particular series is the case of the Luscombe 8 line. Many of the early models in the series, particularly the 8-A had a fuel tank in the fuselage aft of the pilot's seat. Later models such as the 8-E and 8-F have one or more wing tanks instead of the fuselage tank. Naturally, the wing tanks will raise the C.G. to a level somewhat higher than the fuselage tank when filled. The elevated C.G. will result in a greater likelihood of nose-over upon heavy application of brakes.

SIDE AREA OF FUSELAGE AND VERTICAL TAIL

The size of the vertical tail and the area of the fuselage side are significant contributors to a taildragger's weathercocking tendency. This will not be felt in the air, but will be important from the moment the main gear touches the ground during a crosswind landing. The larger the vertical tail surface, the more the weathercocking. For the sake of comparison, the Piper J-3 Cub and the Taylorcraft BC-12 series both represent designs with relatively small fuselage side surface areas. On the other hand, one of their contemporaries, the Aeronca 7AC Champ sports a fuselage reminiscent of a pregnant guppy, and requires additional amounts of control in a strong crosswind.

In a similar fashion, the amount of dihedral in a given design will add to the control difficulty in a crosswind. The more the dihedral, the more the wind will succeed in getting under the wing to exert a lifting influence just when the pilot doesn't want it. The price of dihedral is that the pilot will have to perform more wing lowering for a given crosswind than might otherwise have been required. And again, the Aeronca Champ with considerably more dihedral than the Cub or Taylorcraft, is a good example.

RUDDER SIZE, DISPLACEMENT, AND EFFECTIVENESS

Rudder size, amount of travel, and effectiveness all play an important part in the airplane's ability to handle crosswinds. Note the distinction. It is the airplane's ability which we are concerned with here, and not the pilot's. Regardless of the pilot's particular expertise, he will, in some models be restricted by rudder limits. This will reduce the amount of crosswind in which he can safely operate. If he is highly experienced in the breed, this limit will be well known and is not likely to present a serious problem. On the other hand, if the pilot has little time in type, he may not discover the crosswind limit until he is on final to the only runway within remaining fuel range and suddenly realizes that the right rudder pedal all the way to the firewall is insufficient to compensate for the wind. This is not the time nor place to make such a discovery. Examples of models in this category are the Globe/Temco Swift and the Bellanca Cruisair series.

If you feel that there is insufficient rudder effectiveness in your particular favorite bird, don't despair. See your friendly A&P or IA, and have him examine the specifications for the airplane, and the airplane itself. It could be that the control stops or control rigging have been incorrectly adjusted in the past, and that subsequent annual inspections which should have caught this deficiency haven't.

If the problem were caused by the stops being incorrectly set, it would be very easy to correct. On the other hand, if the problem is the result of improper control and control cable rigging, the situation will require a bit more time to resolve. This is very likely if the airplane is a particularly old bird for which rigging instructions may be scarce or unavailable.

ELEVATOR CONTROL

What appears to be a minor example of differences between models of the same type is the elevator control in the Cessna 170 series. The earlier models in the series, the 170 and the 170A were devoid of counterweights in the aerodynamic balance sections of the elevator. Consequently, the force of gravity pulls the elevators down when the airplane is at rest. While this might appear inconsequential to the reader, it does result in the requirement for a great deal of force to achieve the proper amounts of back-elevator for three-point landings. This is especially the case when the pilot flies solo with a minimum fuel load thus giving a forwardmost C.G.. This problem was recognized by Cessna, and lead weights were added to the aerodynamic balance sections of the elevator on the 170B (Ref.8). While this should not be looked on as a serious problem, it could add to the surprise factor for a pilot experienced in the "B" model who flies an

"A" or earlier model for the first time. Imagine his discomfiture as he attempts three-pointers and cannot understand the source of his difficulty in getting the tail all the way down.

BRAKES

The brake considerations take on much more importance for a taildragger than they normally would for the typical tricycle geared airplane. To begin with, the type of wheel brake used may be important in terms of reliability and maintenance. For example, we find that two makes of brakes equip a large number of the taildragger fleet. These are the Goodyear, and the Cleveland types, and their derivatives. The Cleveland brake has been added to a large number of airplanes as an "after market" product, and seems to be more easily maintained than its Goodyear counterpart. This simple attribute may be important because a brake more easily maintained may mean that it is more likely to be maintained. See additional comments concerning brake maintenance in the MAINTENANCE section of this chapter.

A second important brake consideration is the type of brake pedal with which the airplane is equipped. The commonly seen types are the "Heel" and the "Toe" brakes. Many taildragger pilots would have us believe that Heel brakes are a nightmare creator of Hitchcockian proportions. The general idea that heel brakes are difficult or even dangerous to use is a belief held by pilots who haven't much experience with them. This is folklore! Let's not forget that most of the light airplanes built before WW-II were equipped with these exciting devices (assuming that they had brakes in the first place) and that thousands of pilots received their flight training in them. To be sure, we are referring to an era in which pilots did not expect to find "automobile" type brakes in their airplanes. Indeed, many did not expect any brakes at all. During this time frame, there were still significant numbers of airplanes sold without brakes of any kind. Hence, the pilot of a brake equipped airplane was likely to be happy with the availability of brakes and unlikely to complain because the brakes were to be operated with the heels. Let's also note that the mechanical brakes with which most of the older airplanes were equipped were not easy to maintain and to keep properly adjusted. Therefore, much of the undeserved bad reputation of Heel brakes stems from attempted use of poorly maintained hardware.

While it is true that Heel brakes are slightly more difficult to use than the Toe version, they are still usable with ease and safety if the pilot will first take the time to get accustomed to the location of the pedals and the heel motions which will be required. This is best accomplished while taxiing in an unconstrained area where space exists for mistakes. In this respect, lady pilots would be well advised to not try this game while wearing high-heeled shoes. Note, that in the two seat tandem airplanes, the positioning of the brake pedals may not be the same for the front versus the rear seat. Hence, the pilot who has just switched seats should take the time to re-acquaint himself with the positioning of the brake controls.

Toe brakes are generally a bit easier to use, and are more likely to be a familiar device to the transitioning pilot (unless all of his previous flight experience has been in hand-brake equipped Cherokees). To that extent, use of them will be quicker and safer. It would, however, be foolish to believe that Toe brakes are so safe as to preclude the possibility of problems associated with their use. The following anecdote will serve as an example.

The author had been engaged in administering dual to a number of pilots who had formed a club centered around a newly purchased Luscombe 8-E. As luck would have it, this model had been equipped with toe brakes, and no unusual difficulties were anticipated nor experienced. That is until the fateful day in which one of the pilots requested that the instructor give her young son a ride in the airplane. (She had promised him a ride and was unable to give it herself because her check-out was still incomplete). Our gallant CFI said "sure" and promptly taxied out with his young passenger and within seconds had nearly put the airplane on its nose due to over-confidence and lack of familiarity. Lack of familiarity only because all of his time in this airplane had been in the right seat while giving dual, and this flight was his first in the left seat, the side with the brakes. The near disaster occurred as he approached the take-off end of the grass runway while back-taxiing for takeoff and hastily braked to a stop for execution of the pre take-off checklist and to clear traffic. During the sudden brake application, my size 11 boot became wedged between the tip of the toe brake and the hot air duct against the firewall. This caused the tail to rise to waist level until I was able to extricate my foot and recover without damage but with an additional measure of gray hair. This unscheduled excitement could have been averted had the instructor taken the time to acquire a feel for the brakes. This action would surely have made him notice the proximity of the air duct, and with it the potential for conflict. This experience was related only to point out that Toe brakes don't guarantee immunity from brake actuation problems.

At this point, we will digress for a moment to highlight a potential problem concerning brakes as it applies in a taildragger check-out program. Many of the taildraggers in existence have brake pedals only for the left seat and none for the right. This leaves the instructor with the choice of sitting on the left with access to the brakes, or occupying the right seat and trusting to the student's use of the brakes. The judicious instructor will probably opt for a little bit of each, by beginning the transition while on the left side and in command of the brakes, and then moving to the right seat once he has proved to himself that the student can be trusted to use the correct amount of brakes at the right time.

Finally, let's not forget that there are other types of brake control in addition to the aforementioned Heel or Toe brakes. Some of these can be found in the older classics and in strange Warbird types. A couple of examples suffice to alert the reader to their existence and to convince him that any strange type of brake mechanism should be approached with caution and only after having been enlightened with the proper "care and feeding" instructions. The Beechcraft C-17 series Staggerwings were built with brakes controlled by a hand actuated handle. It was said of these airplanes that the pilot needed three hands to make a landing. The later D-17 series sported toe brakes which no doubt increased the happiness quotient among pilots (Ref. 5). Other examples of strange brake actuation devices are the British Spitfire and the DeHavilland Mosquito, both of which make use of a hand actuated lever on the control column to activate the brake, with braking taking place on the side on which the rudder pedal is depressed. If the rudder control is in neutral, then both brakes are applied equally (Ref. 9).

SHOCK ABSORBERS

The light taildraggers which we've been discussing and which are often the reason for a taildragger transition have varied means of absorbing the shock in the landing gear. These span the spectrum from the delightful long stroke shock absorbers used on the Waco UPF-7 to "none" as in the case of many lightweight home-builts. In between these two extremes, we have the Cessna 120/140/170/-180/190 with spring steel gear giving very little shock absorption, and the Piper J-3/J-4/J-5/PA-11/PA-12's which are equipped with Piper's trademark, the bungee shock absorber, also known in some circles as a "built-in slingshot". The Cessna spring steel gear can be the cause of a disconcerting side to side rocking motion, which if allowed to build unchecked can cause a departure for the bushes during the landing roll-out.

The bungee found on the typical Pipers mentioned can be the source of harder landings than those of airplanes equipped with true shock absorbing devices. Continuing our earlier comparison of the Piper J-3 with the Aeronca 7AC Champ, we find that this is an area where the little Champ really shines. Its simple shock absorber of "near automobile" type has always been the source of pleasing "grease jobs" for landings.

The importance of the foregoing description to the typical pilot is to alert him to the potential differences between types and encourage him to learn as much about them as he can.

INDIVIDUAL PREFERENCES

As the taildragger pilot gains experience in various models, he will learn that quite a few have individual preferences with respect to handling. In some cases, these preferences stem from design problems which left a component or other with some level of weakness which could be the cause of maintenance problems if ignored.

Our first example used to demonstrate this point is the Globe/Temco Swift. This airplane is generally wheel landed by its owners in order to avoid the three-point landing which tends to be more difficult and unpredictable to achieve smoothly than in the more benign taildragger. Hence, it is wise to avoid full stall landings in this airplane.

The second example is the Cessna L-19 Bird Dog. In this airplane the three-point landing can be accomplished quite smoothly albeit often accompanied with a side to side rocking motion. However, the airplane is prone to damage of the tail wheel mechanism by unusually hard landings which slam the tail wheel to the ground. Should our pilot ignore this problem, the price will be continuous replacement of the tail wheel mechanisms and tail springs. This is the price paid by the U.S. Army for its cruel and abusive treatment of Bird Dogs at Ft. Rucker. This isn't intended as a criticism of the Army, because this treatment was required in the training of Army pilots for typical conditions under hostile fire.

Our final example is of the Cessna 120 through 195 series using the spring steel gear. As farfetched as it may seem, these airplanes can be subjected to hard wheel landings of such intensity that the gear will temporarily spread apart sufficiently to allow the propeller to strike the ground. The gear will then spring back to its original spacing leaving the pilot with a strange look on his face as he views the curled propeller tips after engine shutdown.

MAINTENANCE

Pilots in general tend to fly hardware with known deficiencies a lot more often than they should. Usually, this action takes place because of haste, and is repeated only because the pilot "got away with it" last time. Our tricycle geared airplanes are very forgiving in the face of such foolishness. Examples are flying with one brake inoperative, or with one under-inflated main tire. For the pilot to bring such foolhardy habits to taildragger flying would be flirting with disaster. In this section we will discuss examples of maintenance items which might not cause an accident if neglected in a tricycle geared airplane, but which may well be the cause of a major catastrophe in a taildragger. This is not intended as an exhaustive list, but will be long enough to show how airplane types can be so different from each other. The reader can then use his imagination with respect to all the other types not mentioned here, and may wisely decide that counsel should be sought from people (pilots and mechanics) who know their particular breed of interest well.

ITEMS OF GENERAL APPLICABILITY (Independent of make or model).

A. **Brakes.** The pilot who flies a taildragger with one or more inoperative brakes is in for an exciting time, and sooner or later this practice will lead to a disaster. Murphy's second law of taildraggers is that the crosswind will be from the side opposite the inoperative brake. And while a pilot can fly a tricycle geared airplane (depending on the make and model) without one of its brakes, it is usually due to the fact that the trigear is positively steered via the nose wheel, and that the airplane may be stopped by a single working brake without veering off in that direction. This is aided by the action of the nose wheel which stabilizes the airplane directionally. In the taildragger case, an attempt at stopping with only one brake will generally initiate a sharp turn, because the tail wheel does not provide the stabilizing influence which a nose wheel would have. Indeed, if it is of the castering type, it will be useless for this purpose. If it is of the steerable/full swivel type, the application of brake on one side will probably force it beyond the steerable range into full swivel. Of course, if the tail wheel is of the lockable type, it should be locked to assist in coping with this problem.

B. **Tail Wheel.** The tail wheel should be given proper maintenance emphasizing proper lubrication and attachment and health of the steering springs and cables. An occasional ground check to assure proper steering and castering is worth the slight time involved. The author recalls a moment of extreme embarrassment when he persisted in flying his Cessna 170 beyond the point where damage to the swivel mechanism had been recognized, and attempted repairs had proved unsuccessful. The occasion occurred at the moment prior to take-off when an attempt was made to taxi onto the short, narrow, snow bank bounded grass runway. When the tail wheel refused to go into the full swivel mode on the right hand side, the airplane was unable to negotiate the sharp turn required. The pilot was left with only one option, that being to shut down the engine, and push the tail around by hand. Once was enough to convince the author that $350. for a new tail wheel would be money well spent.

C. **Tires.** Tires should be inflated to their recommended level, and particular care should be taken to insure that the inflation level is the same in both main tires. The pilot doesn't need the handicap of steering the taildragger with one low tire.

D. **Tail Wheel Locking Mechanism.** If the airplane is so equipped, remember that the designer incorporated it there for good reason. It should therefore be kept in operating condition, and should be maintained to assure that it isn't so worn as to become useless. Some tail wheel locks are sufficiently worn to allow the tail wheel a castering range of 10 to 20 degrees. This is enough to cause considerable grief on the take-off roll.

E. **Cross Wind Gear.** The need for proper maintenance of the Cross Wind Gear and its locking mechanism (if present) was mentioned in Chapter 8, and is repeated here as a reminder. The inspection of the locking pins should be made a preflight inspection check-list item.

ITEMS PERTAINING TO SPECIFIC MAKES OR MODELS

A. **Cessna Series.** It is very important that the main gear be properly "shimmed", and preferably by a mechanic experienced in this procedure. Improper shimming is often difficult to detect and may contribute to an accident, especially if the pilot has a low experience level in taildraggers. Improper shimming may be detected by having a couple of helpers push the airplane by hand down the center line of a smooth paved taxi way, and positioning an observer twenty to thirty feet ahead of the airplane in order to watch the behavior of the gear. If the separation between the main wheels gradually decreases (or increases), it will do so to the point that spring action will quickly restore it to its original spacing with a sudden "twang". The effect of this during a wheel landing is bound to be exciting, to say the least.

B. **deHavilland Beaver.** The Beaver's tail wheel tire comes equipped with ridges at the extreme edge of the tire, symmetrically about the tire's center line. These ridges are important in eliminating tail wheel shimmy. Once the tires are worn to the extent that the ridges are level with the remainder of the tire, the tire must be discarded and replaced. Attempts at continued use beyond this point will result in extreme tail wheel shimmy with accompanying severe vibration of the entire structure. A similarly ridged tire is also used on the tail wheel of many versions of the North American T-6 "Texan".

Flaps. A second important maintenance item for the Beaver is Flaps. A take-off should not be attempted in a Beaver with inoperative flaps (flaps which cannot be lowered to the "take-off" position) due to the excessive runway length which will be required. The reason for this is that a Beaver, in a three-point attitude with flaps raised, has insufficient angle of attack to create much lift. In a normal take-off with flaps lowered to the "take-off" position, the lowered flaps along with the lowered ailerons serve to dramatically increase the angle of attack, and this is the source of the Beaver's outstanding performance. This also serves to notify the reader of the importance of check-list use. If the flaps are forgotten, it is immaterial whether they are operative or not. The net result will be a greatly increased takeoff run (assuming the presence of a runway of sufficient length).

C. **Maule Tail wheels.** Airplanes with Maule tail wheels (and bear in mind that many taildraggers do have them, not just Maule taildraggers) require attention to the tail wheel steering springs. If shimmy problems are to be avoided, the springs must be deliberately mis-matched in terms of strength. Hence we have the possible scenario of the unwitting owner who notices that one of his springs is corroded and decides to replace it. If he decides to buy one of the same strength as on the other side (which would be the wrong thing to do), he will wonder why the tail wheel has now developed a significant shimmy.

APPENDIX A

EXCERPTS OF PERTINENT FAR'S

EXCERPTS OF PERTINENT FEDERAL AVIATION
REGULATIONS [1]

Paragraph 61.31 **General Limitations**

(g) *Tailwheel Airplanes.* No person may act as pilot in command of a tailwheel airplane unless that pilot has received flight instruction from an authorized flight instructor who has found the pilot competent to operate a tailwheel airplane and has made a one time endorsement so stating in the pilot's logbook. The endorsement must certify that the pilot is competent in normal and crosswind takeoffs and landings, wheel landings unless the manufacturer has recommended against such landings, and go-around procedures. This endorsement is not required if a pilot has logged flight time as

---

[1] The regulations quoted above (except for Par. 61.31 (g) which is from Reference 18) are those currently in force at the end of the 1990 calendar year. They were taken from Reference 10. At any future time, it is suggested that the reader refer to the equivalent current regulations.

pilot in command of tailwheel airplanes prior to April 15, 1991.

Paragraph 61.57 **Recent Flight Experience: pilot in command.**

(a) ....

(b) ....

(c) *General experience.* No person may act as pilot in command of an aircraft carrying passengers, nor of an aircraft certificated for more than one required pilot flight crew member, unless within the preceding 90 days, he has made three takeoffs and three landings as the sole manipulator of the flight controls in an aircraft of the same category and class and, if a type rating is required, of the same type. If the aircraft is a tailwheel airplane, the landings must have been made to a full stop in a tailwheel airplane.

For the purpose of meeting the requirements of the paragraph a person may act as pilot-in-command of a flight under day VFR or day IFR if no persons or property other than as necessary for his compliance thereunder, are carried. This paragraph does not apply to operations requiring an airline transport pilot-certificate, or to operations conducted under Part 135 of this chapter.

(d) ....

(e) ....

Paragraph 61.191 **Additional flight instructor ratings.**

The holder of a flight instructor certificate who applies for an additional rating on that certificate must -

(a) Hold an effective pilot certificate with ratings appropriate to the flight instructor rating sought.

(b) Have had at least 15 hours as pilot in command in the category and class of aircraft appropriate to the rating sought.

(c) Pass the written and practical test prescribed in this subpart for the issuance of a flight instructor certificate with the rating sought.

Paragraph 61.195 **Flight instructor limitations.**

(a) ....

(b)......

(c) ....

(d) ....

(e) ....

(f) *Instruction in multiengine airplane or helicopter.* He may not give flight instruction required for the issuance of a certificate or a category, or class rating, in a multiengine airplane or a helicopter, unless he has at least five hours of experience as pilot in command in the make and model of that airplane or helicopter, as the case may be.

Paragraph 91.109 **Flight instruction; Simulated instrument flight and certain flight tests.**

(a) No person may operate a civil aircraft (except a manned free balloon) that is being used for flight instruction unless that aircraft has fully functioning, dual controls. However, instrument flight instruction may be given in a single-engine airplane equipped with a single, functioning throwover control wheel in place of fixed, dual controls of the elevator and ailerons, when—

(1) The instructor has determined that the flight can be conducted safely; and

(2) The person manipulating the controls has at least a private pilot certificate with appropriate category and class ratings.

APPENDIX B

ANALYSIS OF P-FACTOR

The development of left-turning tendency due to P-Factor, known in some circles as *torque*, is to many pilots and flight instructors alike somewhat of a ghost phenomena. The normally given explanation for this inconvenience is that *it is due to asymmetric loading of the propellor blades due to the fact that the descending blade has a greater angle of attack than the ascending blade.* While this explanation is technically correct, it is far from clear, and leaves the questioner with the fundamental question *how can that be, since, in a fixed pitch prop, both blades are "welded" at the same angle?* Even the better aviation text books provide only this cursory explanation without daring to venture into the morass of mathematics which would be needed to provide additional insight. This leads the reader to suspect that the author doesn't really understand the phenomena any better than the student does, and that it was included in the book only because the author copied from an earlier text.

The purpose of this appendix is to show that there is indeed a mathematical basis to this claim, and to proceed with an example based on measurements made on a real airplane so that the reader can have the benefit of a numerical result. The reader can then judge whether this phenomena is truly significant or nothing more than an interesting triviality.

B   THE COMPLEAT TAILDRAGGER PILOT

A final objective must be that we minimize the mathematics used in the explanation thus making it useful to the pilot who is not equipped with an engineering degree. To this end, we have minimized the number of equations, supplied all the intermediate steps which scientific texts generally leave for the reader to prove, and added numerous diagrams which are usually easier to follow than are pure mathematical theorems. Those who feel inclined can follow each step in the development of the example, while readers without this level of interest or ability may skim the detailed material or ignore it entirely and proceed directly to the results at the end of this appendix.

ANALYSIS

We begin by introducing some general material and will then proceed to an example involving actual measurements on a typical taildragger. From this, we will calculate the difference in thrust exerted by equivalent sections of two identical propeller blades, one which is ascending—on the left side of the airplane, and one which is descending.

The first item needed is the general equation for lift presented here as Equation B-1. This equation applies to any low speed airfoil, of which a propeller blade is an example. Available from any standard aerodynamics text[1], we have:

---

[1] See Reference 1 in the Reference Section at the end of this book.

$$L = C_L \times \frac{\rho}{2} \times S \times V^2 \qquad \text{B-1}$$

which reminds us that lift, given by L, is proportional to S which represents the airfoil area, C_L which is the coefficient of lift for the airfoil in question, and the square of velocity. ρ is the standard symbol for air density. If we then assume that the density is constant and that the airfoil will be operated in a region where the coefficient of lift is a fairly linear function of angle of attack, we may replace all the variables except angle of attack and velocity by a constant, and re-write equation B-1 to read:

$$L = K \times \alpha \times V^2 \qquad \text{B-2}$$

which is the most important equation for our purposes. An examination of this equation shows that lift on a given blade section is dependent on K which is a constant of proportionality, α, which is the angle of attack (of the blade element in question), and the velocity, V, squared. We will now examine the dynamics of the airflow as it impinges on the ascending and descending blades to determine the differences in angle of attack and velocity if any.

In Figure B-1 we see that the blade section which we've chosen to analyze is at a radius of 26 inches, which for a 76 inch diameter propeller is near the 75 percent radius where the blade angle of fixed pitch propellers is customarily measured. Figure B-2a shows the propeller plane of rotation as vertical for the typical tricycle geared airplane, whereas Figure B-2b shows it tilted at 11 degrees representing the value for the Cessna 170 taildragger. Both the tilt angle, T, of 11 degrees and the pitch angle of 19 degrees were obtained from actual measurements made on the author's 170 and will be used for our first example.

The diagrams in Figure B-3 show the blade angle relationships for a tricycle geared airplane at rest. Note that the

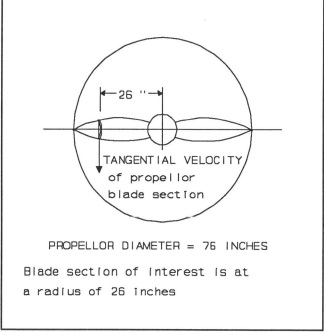

Figure B-1 Propellor blade section used in our calculations

propeller plane of rotation is vertical as we would expect. Also note that the angle of attack is the same for either blade, and is equal to

$$V = \frac{RPM \times 2 \times 3.14 \times R \times 60}{12 \times 5280} \qquad \text{(B-3)}$$

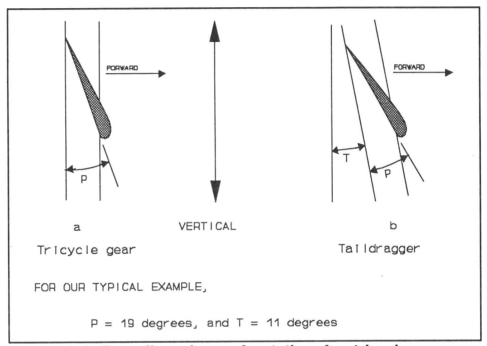

Figure B-2 Propellor plane of rotation for tricycle gear vs. taildragger

the pitch angle P. The RPM value of 2300 chosen for this example is typical of the Cessna 170 or 172 with a Continental O-300 engine. In either of these diagrams, the tangential velocity of the air at the chosen blade section during static run-up (no forward velocity) is identical, and can be calculated using equation B-3. For the rpm and blade section distance given above, the result is 355.6 miles per hour

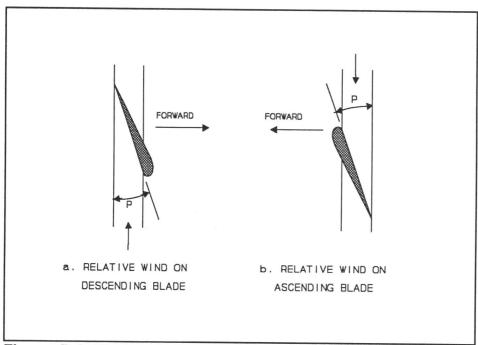

Figure B-3 Blade relative wind for tricycle gear at rest (no forward motion)

as shown in equation B-4.

For a taildragger, the propeller plane of rotation is tilted from the vertical by some angle depending on the design of the particular

$$V = \frac{2300 \; x \; 2 \; x \; 3.14 \; x \; 26 \; x \; 60}{12 \; x \; 5280} = 355.6 \; mph \qquad \text{(B-4)}$$

airplane and conditions i.e. the amount of air in the tires, etc., as is shown in Figure B-4. In our case, the tilt angle is 11 degrees as previously mentioned. In Figures B-4a and b, note that, as the propeller plane of rotation was tilted with respect to the vertical, the relative wind was also tilted by the same amount thereby remaining in the plane of rotation. Hence, for the case of no forward motion, the angle of attack on each blade is still equal. This confirms that there is no P-factor when the airplane is at rest, even though the engine is at full power, regardless of whether it is a taildragger or tricycle gear.

Because the plane of rotation is tilted with respect to the vertical, it becomes useful to show the relative wind as made up of horizontal and vertical components, or vectors. This is shown relatively in Figures B-4 and B-5, and the values can be calculated using equations B-5 and B-6.

$$V_h = 355.6 \; X \; Sin(11°) = 67.8mph \qquad \text{(B-5)}$$

$$V_v = 355.6 \; x \; Cosin(11°) = 349 \; mph \qquad \text{(B-6)}$$

These will be useful as we continue our analysis and the notion of horizontal and vertical components of velocity will be carried through the remaining diagrams.

Figure B-6 is where we begin seeing the effects of forward motion. In this example, we've chosen the value of 40 mph at which to calculate the asymmetric loading. This corresponds to the approximate point in the takeoff run where the pilot will raise the tail. This then (just prior to raising the tail) is the point where P-factor will have reached its maximum value (it represents the peak of the curve in Figure 5.1b of Chapter 5).

This forward velocity of 40 mph is then added in vector form to the existing air velocities. This is shown in Figure B-6. We next proceed to Figures B-7 and B-8 which are nothing more than Figures B-6a and b expanded to improve visibility into the important variables.

$$V_{td} = \sqrt{V_h^2 + V_v^2} = \sqrt{107.8^2 + 349^2} = 365.4 \; mph \qquad \text{(B-7)}$$

An examination of the velocity vectors for the descending blade (Figure B-7), shows that the airplane's forward velocity of 40 mph. is added to the existing horizontal of velocity of 67.8 mph. giving a total horizontal air flow of 107.8 mph. If we now vectorially combine the horizontal and vertical components to obtain the total velocity, the result is represented by the solid vector whose length can be calculated by equation B-7, with a resulting value of 365.4 mph. Before leaving Figure B-7 we note that the angle of the total wind vector has been increased by this forward motion as shown by angle ϕ.

In a similar manner, we examine Figure B-8 for the ascending blade. Here the

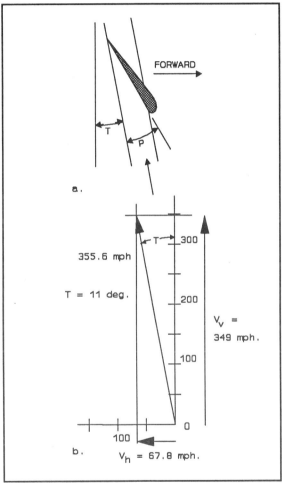

Figure B-4 Air striking the descending blade—taildragger at rest

forward velocity of 40 mph. is subtracted from the horizontal velocity of 67.8 mph. leaving 27.8 mph. in the horizontal direction. As in the previous case, these components of velocity can be combined to obtain the total velocity. This is done using equation B-8, and we obtain a result of 350.2 mph. represented by the solid vector as shown in Figure B-8.

Note that in this case, the angle of the total wind vector has been <u>decreased</u> by the addition of forward motion, which is the opposite of the effect on the other blade. Likewise, the total blade velocity has also been decreased by forward motion. This is a significant result, especially so since the authors of the existing texts make no mention of the velocity

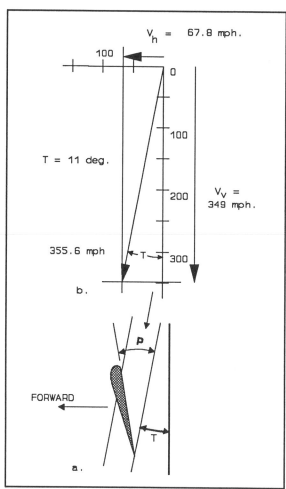

Figure B-5 Air striking the ascending blade—taildragger at rest

$$V_{ta} = \sqrt{27.8^2 + 349^2} = 350.2 \ mph \qquad \text{(B-8)}$$

difference as a potential source of differential thrust resulting in the left-turning tendency called P-factor.

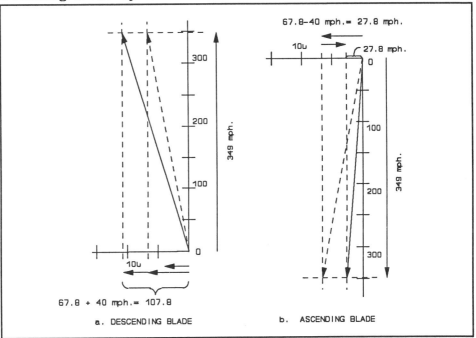

Figure B-6 Relative wind on taildragger in motion

We now return to Figures B-7 and B-8 in order to calculate the exact value of angle ϕ, the angle of the total wind vector. This angle is

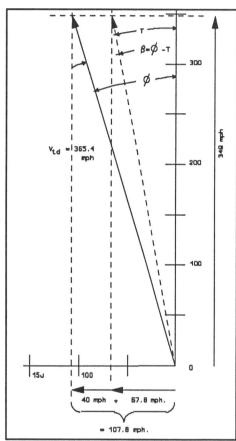

Figure B-7 Angle relationships-descending blade

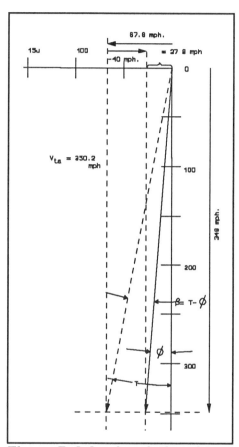

Figure B-8 Angle relationships-ascending blade

found using the relationship in equation B-9 for the descending blade, and equation B-10 for its ascending partner.

$$\phi_d = ATAN \frac{107.8}{349} = 17.17° \quad\quad (B\text{-}9)$$

$$\phi_a = ATAN \frac{27.8}{349} = 4.56° \quad\quad (B\text{-}10)$$

Our next step is to calculate angle β for each case. These are easily found using the definitions shown in Figures B-7 and B-8. For the example of the descending blade, we have

$$\beta_d = \phi_d - T = 17.17° - 11° = 6.17° \quad\quad (B\text{-}11)$$

whereas for the ascending blade,

$$\beta_a = T - \phi_a = 11° - 4.56° = 6.44° \quad\quad (B\text{-}12)$$

We note here that neither of the angles calculated thus far represent the angle of attack which is our goal. Rather, the angles just calculated are simply important steps on the way to finding the angle of attack. How do we know this? Very simply. We worked backwards from the figures that follow.

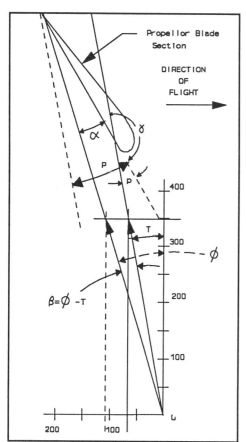

Figure B-9 Angular construct to determine α - descending blade

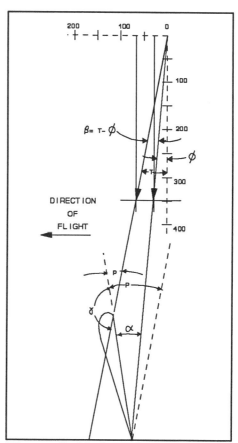

Figure B-10 Angular construct to determine α - ascending blade

Let's proceed to Figures B-9 and B-10 in which the vector diagrams of the air flow have been overlaid with the airfoil and propeller plane geometry. In other words, Figure B-4a representing the airfoil in the rotating propellor plane has been aligned with the air velocity vector from Figure B-7 in order to form Figure B-9. The result is a geometrical configuration which helps us visualize the solution. In Figure B-9, we immediately see that angle α is our elusive angle of attack, and that we must solve the triangle formed by the solid lines in order to obtain its value. Everything else in this diagram is extraneous but has been retained to show the development of the solution. We also note that angle p is identical to the pitch angle P. It is drawn as a separate angle only to serve as a visual aid to our solution. Figure B-10 was created in a similar manner for the ascending blade.

With an understanding of how the diagrams in Figures B-9 and B-10 originated, we can now simplify them by stripping out most of the extraneous lines, leaving only bare bones of the problem to be solved. This results in Figures B-11 and B-12 (each of these 2 figures contains an inset to assist in deciphering the angles shown). In Figure B-11, angle γ is given by equation B-13.

$$\gamma = 180° - p = 180° - 19° = 161° \qquad \text{(B-13)}$$

The angle of attack can be obtained by solving the triangle formed by the solid lines, with the final solution being given by equation B-14 for the descending blade.

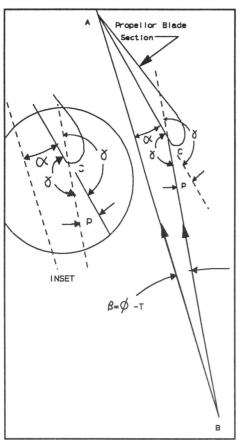

Figure B-11 Triangle solution for α - descending blade

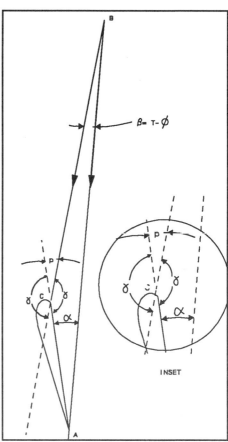

Figure B-12 Triangle solution for α - ascending blade

$$\alpha_d = 180° - \gamma - \beta_d \qquad \text{(B-14)}$$
$$= 180° - 161° - 6.17° = 12.83°$$

When we substitute into this equation the proper values for our example, the resulting angle of attack is found to be 12.83 degrees.

For the case of the ascending blade, we proceed to Figure B-12 and find that equations B-11 and B-12 still apply in principle, and by substituting the proper value for β ($\beta_a = 6.44$ from equation B-12), we obtain

$$\alpha_a = 180° - \gamma - \beta_a \qquad \text{(B-15)}$$
$$= 180° - 161° - 6.44° = 12.56°$$

a value of 12.56 degrees for the angle of attack.

RESULTS

On the surface, it may appear to the reader that this entire exercise has been a complete waste of time, since in either case the angles of attack for ascending and descending blades are *nearly* the same as are their respective relative velocities. However, it would be foolish to give up after having progressed this far. Indeed, it would be useful to summarize our progress to date in order to see the direction in which we should continue. This summary is in Table B-1.

	Descending Blade	Ascending Blade
Angle of Attack	12.83 deg.	12.56 deg.
Relative Velocity	365.4 mph	350.2 mph

Table B-1 Blade section air flow for Cessna 170

Note from Table B-1 that the descending blade has both a higher angle of attack, and a greater relative velocity. If we now continue under the assumptions given earlier in this Appendix, we can use equation B-2 to look at the final results. Restating it here:

$$L = K \times \alpha \times V^2 \qquad \text{(B-2)}$$

we can insert the values for one blade and then for the other, obtaining:

$$L_d = K \times 12.83° \times (365.4 \ mph.)^2 \qquad \text{(B-16)}$$

for the descending blade, and

$$L_a = K \times 12.56° \times (350.2 \ mph.)^2 \qquad \text{(B-17)}$$

for the ascending one. Since we are looking for the difference in the lift from opposing blades, we need not solve equations B-16 and B-17 for the final value of L_d and L_a, and therefore don't need to know the value of K, our constant of proportionality. This simplifies our task considerably.

If we now divide equation B-16 by equation B-17, the result is the ratio of relative thrust for the two blades as shown in equation B-18.

$$\frac{L_d}{L_a} = \frac{12.83° \ x \ (365.4 \ mph.)^2}{12.56° \ x \ (350.2 \ mph.)^2} \qquad \text{(B-18)}$$
$$= 1.11$$

Hence, we've shown that the thrust for small sections of propeller blade equidistant from the center is 11 per cent greater for the descending blade. This is a striking result. If the descending blade is, on the average, producing 11% more thrust than the ascending blade, is it any wonder why the taildragger wants to veer to the left and requires so much right rudder to keep it on the center line.

A second example is used just to show that the differences obtained above were not due to coincidence. For this example, the Cessna L-19 Birddog is used with angle T equal to 10.5 degrees, while the pitch angle, P, is measured at a radius of 38 inches and is equal to 12.5 degrees. When we insert these values into equations B-3 onward, we obtain the values shown in Table B-2. Substituting these values into equations B-5 and B-6 and then obtaining the lift ratio of equation

	Descending Blade	Ascending Blade
Angle of Attack	8.23 deg.	8.11 deg.
Relative Velocity	528.5 mph	513.9 mph

Table B-2 Blade section air flow for Cessna L-19

B-19 which yields:

$$\frac{L_d}{L_a} = \frac{8.23° \; x \; (528.5 \; mph.)^2}{8.11° \; x \; (513.9 \; mph.)^2} \tag{B-19}$$
$$= 1.07$$

Hence the difference in thrust is on the order of 7 % higher for the descending blade. While this is not as dramatic a result as is the 11% figure for the Cessna 170, it is nevertheless a significant one.

We have now achieved our objectives, which were to prove that the angle of attack is indeed different for the ascending and descending blades of a taildragger and to show this without the use of complex mathematics. In addition, we discovered that the blade relative velocities were also different thereby contributing an additional thrust imbalance.

If the preceding development is difficult to accept, bear in mind that pilots in general are not accustomed to thinking in terms of vector equations. Also, the statement that *the descending blade has a higher angle of attack than the ascending blade* is confusing, especially when we speak of a fixed pitch propeller and the pilot knows for a fact that the prop was born with both blades fixed at the same angle. Perhaps the next paragraph will help.

NOTION OF ADVANCING BLADE

Understanding that the concept of different angles of attack and velocities for a descending versus an ascending blade is not easy, but perhaps the difficulty may be eased by thinking in terms of "advancing" and "retreating" blades. Noting that the tilt of the taildragger's propeller plane is a "fore and aft" tilt, the descending blade is seen (in Figure B-4a) to also be advancing with respect to a vertical reference. Likewise, the ascending blade (as seen in Figure B-5a) is moving further toward the rear of the airplane. It is therefore retreating with respect to the direction of flight. Under these circumstances it is a bit more natural to surmise that an advancing blade must be gaining velocity due to the motion of the aircraft, while a retreating blade would be losing velocity. This is exactly what all the vector manipulations have shown. If this appears a bit complex, rest assured that it is. Otherwise, you would have already seen it printed in most aviation texts.

B   THE COMPLEAT TAILDRAGGER PILOT

DIRECTION OF PROPELLER ROTATION

All of the discussion in this appendix has been based on the presence of an American engine (propeller rotation in a clockwise direction as viewed from the cockpit) mounted in a tractor arrangement. Should the engine be of European manufacture which often rotates in the opposite direction (counter-clockwise as seen from the cockpit), all the diagrams would need to be reversed since the ascending and descending blades would have swapped positions to the other side of the airplane. The vector diagrams would be mirror images of the existing ones. All the relationships would be the same (the numerical values would also be the same) except that the final conclusion would be different. The excess thrust would be on the left (descending) propeller blade and the airplane would have a tendency to turn to the right thereby requiring left rudder for compensation.

Another slight perturbation to this analysis should be considered. Namely, what if the engine is mounted in pusher configuration? The answer is that the descending blade is always the one creating the excess thrust provided that the propeller plane is tilted towards the rear as in the typical taildragger configuration (as shown in Figures B-4 and B-5).

Thus an American engine mounted in tractor configuration and a European engine mounted in pusher configuration both develop a left turning tendency. Likewise, a European engine in tractor arrangement and an American engine in a pusher mount would both provide a right turning tendency to the airplane. The use of two engines in push-pull configuration as in the Cessna 337 very neatly cancels out the P-Factor. And as an added bonus, gyroscopic precession is also canceled. Now, if we could cut off the nose wheel and mount one under each tail, wouldn't that make a helluva TTaildragger?

APPENDIX C

ANALYSIS OF THE CRABBED CROSSWIND LANDING

In our discussion of crosswind landings in Chapter 7, we mentioned the Crab type of crosswind landing and its various deficiencies. All too often, the available textbooks don't make it crystal clear that the method doesn't work as advertised, nor do they mention the reasons why this is so.

The purpose of this Appendix is to document the shortcomings of the method, the reasons why the method doesn't do all that is claimed for it (especially as described by the magazine writers on a perennial basis), and to provide an analytical basis for these observations.

DESCRIPTION OF THE CRAB METHOD

Sufficient confusion exists about the Crab method, that we need to spend a bit of time describing exactly what it is that forms the subject of our criticism.

The Crab method of crosswind landing is generally believed to consist of the following:

The final approach is flown in a wings level attitude with the airplane crabbed with respect to the extended runway center line. That is to say that the airplane is progressing on a flight path along or parallel to the extended runway center line. As the airplane is brought closer to the runway, the flare must be performed as it is for any other landing. In this case, the flare is made with the airplane still in a crabbed configuration and, just prior to touchdown, the crab is removed, or the airplane is said to be de-crabbed by the expedient of quickly swinging the nose towards alignment with the runway center line as the airplane touches down. This is accomplished by application of rudder to move the nose in the desired direction, use of ailerons as required to keep the wings level, and a perfect sense of timing. The crabbed and de-crabbed views are shown in Figures 7.1a and b of Chapter 7.

DRAWBACKS OF THE CRAB METHOD

The last item in the above description is the source of our concern and criticism primarily because this "perfect timing" does not exist on a reliably repeatable basis. The perfect timing may exist on a given occasion because you've already made six or eight touch-and-go's and the wind is relatively steady. Thus, you've been able to calibrate the airplane, the pilot, and the environment. Notice that while this was happening, you were flying an airplane with a known load. These are all the right conditions to allow the cultivation of a good sense of timing.

However, ask yourself what will happen to this sense of timing when the pilot makes his first landing of the day during a gusting crosswind at a strange field after a tiring cross-country flight with a full load of passengers. Let's also suppose that our pilot has not landed his airplane with this particular load configuration for two or three months. Do you think he will be able to predict the exact moment of touchdown in a stall landing in order to de-crab right on the money? Hardly!

But why is a perfect sense of timing so important? Some authors have made a point of stating that a perfect sense of timing is not necessary to the success of the method. Indeed, one expert says:

> " *There is a golden moment in the procedure at this point. There is no drift. It's a relatively long moment before drift sets in, and then only gradually at first*" (Ref. 12).

In this statement, the author is incorrect, but first let's establish why "no drift" is desired.

The purpose of any method of landing the airplane in a crosswind is to prevent loss of control or structural failure during the landing and rollout. In general, this is best accomplished by removing or canceling drift at the moment of touchdown. The fact that the landing is in a crosswind is an admission that drift will exist on final unless canceled by the pilot. However, if the method of drift cancellation is not positive, the possibility exists that the temporary cancellation of drift may be followed by a resurgence of drift. Should this happen, the entire maneuver would have been negated since the airplane would now touch down with a drift, which was precisely what the use of the maneuver was to avoid. We can readily see through the description associated with Figures 3.4a and b in Chapter 3, that taildragger drift at touchdown will induce a swing of the nose in the direction of the crosswind, and, if of appreciable velocity, will initiate a ground-loop. Hence, if we haven't canceled the drift, we are not likely to be in control of the airplane much longer.

Indeed the requirement for no drift at touch down is of sufficient importance to convince the FAA to spell it out as a definite criterion applied to the measurement of crosswind landing performance. This is spelled out in the **PRIVATE PILOT PRACTICAL TEST STANDARDS**, Section XI., *Approaches and Landings*, as follows:

> "6. Touches down smoothly at approximate stalling speed, at or within 500 ft beyond a specified point, with no appreciable drift, and the airplane longitudinal axis aligned with the runway centerline."(Ref.14)

BUILD-UP OF DRIFT AFTER DE-CRAB

And now let's return to the remaining question which is "how quickly does drift build up again after the airplane has been de-crabbed in a crosswind".

If we examine the forces acting on the airplane at the exact moment of de-crab, we find only three items of any consequence (bearing in mind that the airplane is still in the air at this time). The first is the force of the crosswind acting on the side area of the fuselage. This is the cause of the drift. Reduce the crosswind to zero, and the drift will remain zero. Likewise, reduce the side area to zero, and we will have no drift. The third ingredient in this puzzle is the weight (mass) of the airplane. The accretion of drift rate will be inversely proportional to the weight. The heavier the airplane, the more slowly it will pick up drift. This is what allows a Boeing 747 to operate in 40 knot crosswind whereas an ultralight might be grounded in one fourth of this crosswind value. The mathematical terms which link the above factors together are of less interest here than the results. Suffice it to say that the relationship of wind velocity, area, and mass is a non-linear one which makes an analytical solution difficult. With the ready availability of today's personal computers however, the non-linear differential equation can be easily solved by means of a rather simple simulation giving us the results shown in Figure C-1.

For our example, the results of which are plotted in Figure C-1, a 15 mph. crosswind was used. Time zero represents the moment of de-crab, and the build up of drift velocity as a function of time is given for three airplanes, the Cessna 170, J-3 Cub, and Douglas DC-3. Note that in 6 seconds, the Cessna 170 has picked up 5 mph. of drift, while in the same time period, the J-3 Cub has re-acquired nearly 7 mph.. As you would expect, the ponderous looking DC-3 has gained less than 2 mph. While it is tempting for the critic to say that a drift of 5 mph is negligible for a Cub or Cessna 170, the only

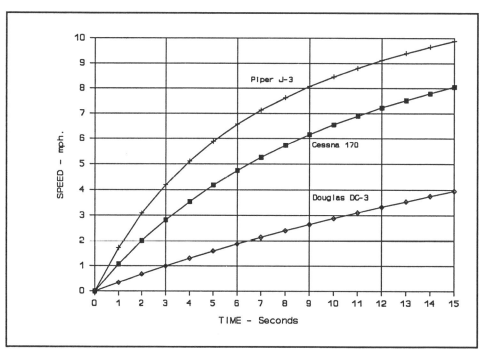

Figure C-1 Re-acquisition of drift speed after De-crab in 15 mph crosswind

critic who will honestly believe this is one who has never landed a J-3 on a hard surface while carrying 5 mph's worth of uncanceled drift. For the case of the DC-3, nearly 25 seconds are required to build up a 5 mph drift. Thus, Collins is perhaps correct, and maybe the DC-3 does have its "golden moment" (in more ways than one).

APPENDIX C
THE CRABBED CROSSWIND LANDING

CONFIRMATION

The reader may easily confirm (within reason) the validity of the calculations leading up to Figure C-1 by the simple expedient of making a crosswind takeoff without crabbing the airplane into the wind after it leaves the ground, and noting how long it takes for a significant drift rate to be noticed. Or, in another fashion, the pilot may make a crabbed crosswind approach all the while prepared for a go-around. At the moment of flare, he kicks the rudder to de-crab the airplane and applies power for the go-around while measuring the time interval between de-crab and appreciable drift. The author's measurements at either of the above tend to be in the range of 3 to 5 seconds for the Cessna 170. Hence, this would tend to confirm by empirical means the data in Figure C-1.

USE OF THE CRAB METHOD

If our previous analysis is correct, and the Crab method is unreliable as applied to light airplanes in general and to light taildraggers in particular, why is the method used at all? And under what conditions is it recommended?

First, if we review the material in Chapter 3 on the comparable stability of the tricycle geared airplane versus that of the taildragger, it is evident that the tricycle gear, because of its inherent stability, can in fact land with a drift without initiating a ground-loop. The proof that this is true is seen at your local airport on each windy day.

C THE COMPLEAT TAILDRAGGER PILOT

It is strongly recommended that the reader spend some time at his favorite airport observing landings on a crosswind day. If the airport is the least bit busy, he will see landings running the gamut from the perfectly executed to the kind with no crosswind correction even attempted. Still, he probably will not witness an accident simply because of the following:

1. The inherent stability of the landing gear configuration will straighten out the tricycle geared airplane touching down with drift.

2. The strength of modern aircraft landing gear is absolutely astounding.

The low accident rate resulting from mal-executed crosswind landings is less of a testimonial to the pilots' skills than to the designer's conservative engineering practices.

Speaking of the use of lowered wing and opposite rudder, no less an authority than Langewiesche tells us in "Stick and Rudder" (Reference 13) that:

> " *This maneuver is admittedly essential in a conventional airplane. But an airplane with tricycle landing gear need not go so strictly straight over the ground at the moment of ground contact; it can afford to touch down with some sideways drift.*"

Hence, pilots continue to use this method of crosswind correction because <u>they can get away with it</u> in tricycle geared airplanes. And this is the reason for such strong emphasis on this point for transitioning pilots. The typical pilot may have built up these bad habits through years of flying tricycle geared airplanes and "getting away with it". The moment he touches down with a 5 mph drift in a taildragger, you can be sure that he will not "get away with it".

Let's also bear in mind that the pilot who follows Langewiesche's dictum and "touches down with some sideways drift", will also be in violation of the Practical Test Standards and will fail the Practical Test.

In fairness to the method however, an examination of Figure C-1 does show that, if the pilot can guess his moment of touch down to within 5 seconds, the 15 mph crosswind will be reduced to a drift of 5 mph. While this may not be considered acceptable for taildragger landings, it is still an improvement over no attempted correction at all.

Still remaining is the question "are there any situations in which the Crab method is indeed recommended?" And the answer is that in the case of a low wing airplane with a long wing span and relatively short landing gear, the Crab may be the only method to use because the low wing method could result in the lowered wing tip or engine pod contacting the ground. In such a case, the pilot has little choice.

A final example of a crabbed crosswind landing being required is for the pilot of the Ercoupe 415 series airplane which has retained its two-control configuration. In this case, without availability of independent rudder control, the airplane must be landed in a crab without the pilot even attempting a de-crab. As specified in the airplane's P.O.H.,

> " 3. Make contact decisively at low speed with plane still crabbed, but **relax grip on control wheel** to allow nose to caster and ease forward on control wheel slowly." (Reference 19)

It is in the diminutive Ercoupe landed in a stiff crosswind that the pilot gains a new appreciation for the term "robust" as applied to landing gear.

Glossary

As in any specialized endeavor, flying and specifically taildragger flying employ words which often have a different and specific meaning when used in this unique context. That meaning may not be obvious or clear to the uninitiated. The purpose of this glossary is to ensure that the terminology used in this book is clear to the reader.

C.G. - Center of Gravity

Crab[1] — Motion of an airplane at some angle with respect to a straight line (usually the runway center line when in the landing configuration). If the nose is pointed to the left of the line of travel, the airplane is said to be "crabbed to the left".

De-crab — Generally associated with the sudden removal of crab during the last moments of a crosswind landing (just prior to touchdown).

Drift — Motion of an airplane with respect to the ground in a direction perpendicular to its longitudinal axis, usually due to wind.

---

[1] Author's note: To the average reader, crab and drift appear to be redundant terms. The difference between the two terms is primarily based on intent. While the term drift is used in the general sense—as in drifting with the wind, crab is used in the specific sense of a predetermined and intentional drift in order to follow a desired trajectory, e.g. an airplane crabbing on final in order for the flight path to follow the runway center line. Whether the airplane touches the ground in a drift or in a crab is academic. The airplane will never know the difference. In this book, the author has used the term crab to indicate a condition in which the pilot has intentionally applied a specific amount of drift meet his objective.

When the airplane's path over a ground reference is to the right of the airplane's longitudinal axis, the airplane is said to be "drifting to the right".

Straight Gear — Refers to ordinary conventional (taildragger) landing gear as compared with Cross Wind Gear in which the main wheels caster within a specified range.

FAA — Federal Aviation Administration

FAA-FSDO — Federal Aviation Administration's Flight Standards District Office

FAA-GADO — Federal Aviation Administration's General Aviation District Office

Full Swivel or Castering tail wheel — Refers to a tail wheel which is non-steerable and which swivels (casters) freely without restraint.

Leeward wing — Wing pointing downwind in a crosswind situation

P.O.H. — Pilot's Operating Handbook refers to the manual normally written by the airplane manufacturer specifying the procedures to be used in flying the airplane safely. This book may exist under a variety of different names, such as: Owner's Manual, Information Manual, Instruction Manual, etc.

Steerable/full swivel tail wheel — Tail wheel which is steerable when within a narrow deflection band about the neutral point. This band may be plus or minus 20 or 30 degrees. Example is the DeHavilland DHC-2 "Beaver" with tail wheel steerable through a range of 25 degrees either side of center(Ref. 4). When this type of tail wheel is forced through a turn (by the brakes and/or rudder) in excess of the steerable amount, it reverts to full swivel operation. It can be returned to steerable operation by taxiing straight until the tailwheel has returned near the center of its steerable range.

Three-point attitude — Attitude of an airplane with respect to the horizon as it sits when parked on level ground.

Windward wing — Wing pointing upwind or into the wind in a crosswind situation

References

1. Aerodynamics for Pilots, by Bradley Jones. Civil Aeronautics Bulletin No. 26, September 1940, U.S. Government Printing Office.

2. Civil Pilot Training Manual, Civil Aeronautics Bulletin No.23, second edition, September 1941. U.S. Government Printing Office.

3. Cross Wind Landing Gear, Civil Aeronautics Administration Contract CAA-24969, Goodyear Aircraft Corporation, Akron, Ohio March 1, 1947.

4. The DeHavilland Beaver Flight Manual, by DeHavilland Aircraft of Canada LTD, Toronto, Ontario. March 1956.

5. U.S.Civil Aircraft, Volume 7 (ATC 601 - ATC 700), by Joseph Juptner. Aero Publishers, Inc. Fallbrook, CA., 1978.

6. U.S.Civil Aircraft, Volume 8 (ATC 701 - ATC 800), by Joseph Juptner. Aero Publishers, Inc. Fallbrook, CA., 1980.

7. The Pilot's Guide to Affordable Classics, by Bill Clarke. TAB Books Inc., Blue Ridge Summit, PA. 1986.

8. The Cessna 170 - Thirty Six Years of A Classic, Published by The International Cessna 170 Association, Hartville, MO. 1984.

9. Pilot's Manual for DeHavilland Mosquito, Air Ministry Publication 2019E-PN, January 1950. Reproduced by Aviation Publications, Milwaukee, WI.

10. FAR 1990 Federal Air Regulations, by TAB/AERO Staff, TAB Books Inc., Blue Ridge Summit, PA. 1990.

11. Flight Training Handbook, Advisory Circular AC 61-21A, U.S. Department of Transportation. Sold by the U.S.Government Printing Office, Washington DC, 20402

12. Takeoffs and Landings, by Leighton Collins, Delacorte Press/Eleanor Friede, New York, N.Y. 1981.

13. Stick and Rudder, by Wolfgang Langewiesche, McGraw-Hill Book Company, New York, N.Y. 1944.

14. Private Pilot Practical Test Standards--FAA-S-8081-1AS, U.S. Department of Transportation, Federal Aviation Administration. Reprinted by ASA Publications Inc., Seattle, WA.

15. Primary Flying, Air Training Command Manual 51-1, September 1952.

16. Owner's Manual, Cessna Model 172 and Skyhawk, Cessna Aircraft Company, Wichita Kansas - 1974.

17. Information Manual, Cessna Model 172P, Cessna Aircraft Company, Wichita Kansas - 1981.

18. Federal Register, Vol. 56, No. 51, 14 CFR Parts 61 and 141, Pilot, Flight Instructor, and Pilot School Certification; Final Rule. March 15, 1991.

19. Ercoupe — Instruction Manual, Engineering and Research Corporation, Riverdale Maryland. Date unknown, probably circa 1946.